As an author and food stylist, Genevieve Taylor splits her time between food writing and creating beautiful food for photography.

She lives in Bristol with her husband and two children, along with her chickens ('the girls'), two dogs and two kittens. *A Good Egg* is loosely based on her blog: **www.genevievetaylor.blogspot.com**

Genevieve is also the author of *STEW!*, *SOUP!* and *Marshmallow Magic*.

A
GOOD
EGG

A YEAR OF RECIPES FROM AN
URBAN HEN-KEEPER

Genevieve Taylor

Photographs by Jason Ingram

eden project books

eden project books

TRANSWORLD PUBLISHERS
61–63 Uxbridge Road, London W5 5SA
A Random House Group Company
www.booksattransworld.co.uk

First published in Great Britain
in 2013 by Eden Project Books
an imprint of Transworld Publishers

A CIP catalogue record for this book
is available from the British Library.

ISBN 978-1-905-81183-0

Addresses for Random House Group Ltd companies outside the UK
can be found at: www.randomhouse.co.uk
The Random House Group Ltd Reg. No. 954009

The Random House Group Ltd makes every effort to ensure that the papers
used in its books are made from trees that have been legally sourced from
well-managed and credibly certified forests. Our paper procurement policy
can be found at:
www.randomhouse.co.uk/paper.htm

Photographs by Jason Ingram
Food styling by Genevieve Taylor
Design by Anthony Cohen
Cover design by Tom Poland/TW

Typeset in Cochin
Printed and bound by Toppan Leefung Printing Limited, China
10 9 8 7 6 5 4 3 2 1

To Rob, for finally saying yes

Acknowledgements

A Good Egg is a book very close to my heart. Creating it has not been just a simple process of writing recipes; it also tells a tale about how my family and I are living our lives. My husband Rob and our beautiful children, Izaac and Eve, deserve my enormous thanks and endless love for letting me share some of our stories. Without their love, not to mention tolerance of my incessant multi-tasking, it would all have been so much harder.

Susanna Wadeson, my editor at Transworld, has been truly wonderful throughout; intuitive, supportive and encouraging. Huge thanks, Susanna, for hearing my 'voice' in a vast sea of others.

Everyone at Transworld has been a great support and *A Good Egg* is a real collaborative effort. To Lynsey Dalladay, my publicist, thanks for your energy and enthusiasm. Thanks to Mari Roberts, my copy editor, for nipping and tucking my words so eloquently. Cover designer Tom Poland, designer Anthony Cohen, design manager Phil Lord and production manager Geraldine Ellison – thank you for making it a thing of beauty as well as practicality.

Big thanks to Kate Hordern, my agent, for all her straight-talking advice and positivity throughout. The beautiful photos of my garden and food were taken by Jason Ingram, a truly talented photographer who was instantly in tune with my vision. Thanks, Jason, for making it all look so delicious.

The germination of many of my recipes starts with distant memories from childhood, and for that my mum deserves many thanks, not to mention a massive hug, for sowing the seeds all those years ago. Friends, old and new, thank you for being willing guinea pigs at my table. Special thanks to Jo Ingleby, my 'cooking buddy', whose knowledge and advice I often seek, but thanks mainly for the wine, the fun and the laughter.

Introduction

I always yearned to keep a few chickens in my back garden. As a passionate animal lover and an enthusiastic eater of good food, I knew a constant fresh supply of eggs, those versatile heroes of the kitchen, would always be put to good use. My husband was rather less keen, and it took me the best part of eight years to persuade him our city garden could be stretched to accommodate a few feathered friends. He was worried about the mess and the commitment, not to mention how they would share the garden with our dogs, cats and children.

As it turned out, everyone muddled along quite well, although the four chickens, the 'girls' as I like to call them, do rather more damage to the garden than I had hoped. Over the course of our first year of hen-keeping we have had to adapt our free-ranging ideals in order for us to have a garden with anything growing at all, and the girls, now very much part of the family, live primarily in an enclosed area that runs long and thin down the length of the garden. They seem quite happy with this arrangement, clucking animatedly every time one of us walks by, particularly the super-noisy Pearl, named for her gorgeous pale grey plumage, who is the only one who likes to be handled. I shan't pretend keeping hens has been entirely straightforward, but the eggs they provide, three or four every day, are truly joyous and worth every penny of the wooden run, the food and the bedding.

A Good Egg charts the year in my kitchen. It is not an egg cookery bible, but rather a seasonal diary of all that I did with my eggs, and the food I grew and gathered to eat alongside them.

The changing seasons are one of the most wonderful things about living in Britain. Like many people who live on this island I like to moan about the weather, but really I relish the change in tempo and mood the seasons bring. Not for me the endless sultry twelve-hour days and nights of the tropics – give me cold frosty mornings and balmy long summer nights any day. I have always been a keen gardener, but now with the arrival of the chickens in my urban plot I have a new and intimate connection to the seasons. Daily forays up and down the garden to feed them scraps from the kitchen and collect the eggs mean that this year, more than ever before, I have been in tune with what is going on outside my back door. And that connection not only makes me feel vital and alive, it has reinvigorated my cooking – and gardening – no end.

Cooking for me is driven by seasonality, simplicity and taste. I am not replicating fancy restaurant food at home, but cooking for pleasure and to provide myself, and my family and friends, with something delicious to eat. And if some of the ingredients – eggs, fruit, vegetables and herbs – come from my garden, the happier I am. I am naturally drawn to the cuisine of the countries around the Mediterranean – Spain, Italy, Turkey, Morocco and Tunisia, in particular – as well as India and the Far East, and so herbs and spices play a vital role in my kitchen. This is due, in no small part, to a love of travel instilled in me as a child by my mum. She ignited a spark of curiosity about the way other people live and eat that still burns bright today, influencing my kitchen, and my kitchen garden.

Growing a few good things to eat brings me immense contentment and satisfaction. I am a working mum so most of my food shopping, out of necessity, happens in a manic trolley dash around the supermarket. But cooking something I have nurtured from seed, protected from frosts, garden pests and over-zealous pets, takes the pleasure I gain from eating to a whole new level. A plate of ripe figs, split open while still warm from the tree, drizzled with olive oil and eaten with creamy ricotta and torn basil leaves was one of my salad highlights of the year. Another triumph was the fat, deeply coloured stems of purple sprouting broccoli, surely the best I have ever eaten, the taste no doubt enhanced by the full twelve months it took to get them from seed to plate. Getting my hands dirty, feeling my way through the soil, adapting our eating to what is available outside, with all the failures and successes, makes me appreciate my food all the more. My children are just as frustratingly fussy as other people's, and would quite happily eat fish fingers slathered in ketchup every day. But I know that by planting and nurturing our own produce, and cooking and eating it with them, in time my children will grow to see the value in good food.

What follows is a record of our year of good eating, from exquisite Portuguese custard tarts in spring to toffee-apple doughnuts around a bonfire in autumn, a warming Malaysian egg curry for a winter night, and a cake for, almost, every weekend of the year. All thanks to the garden, and the girls.

All the eggs I use in these recipes are large, unless otherwise stated.

Spring
A chink of light

Spring is a season of mixed emotions, the weather one day teasing us with a little warm sun, the next day plunging us back into the cold again. Cruelly, snow often seems to come in March, just as we feel we have finally come through the tunnel of another long winter. So eating in spring can be an up-and-down affair, cooking following closely the variable moods of the moment. With the arrival of the chickens I find myself tracking the minute changes in the garden that indicate spring is coming, and this brings me immense joy as I plan for the growing season ahead.

There comes a moment when I finally breathe a quiet sigh of relief, realizing that spring is here: the new season has begun. The flower buds on the magnolia stellata outside my desk window become so plump and fluffy they look like they might burst open at the merest touch. In the woods I spot the first shoots of wild garlic peeping through the woodland floor, tantalizing me with how delicious they will be in a few weeks' time. A little later, the buds on the wisteria have grown and differentiated to the point where I can tell which are going to be leaves and which will turn into precious, headily scented flowers. This, for me, marks the true onset of spring. Change accelerates quickly afterwards.

This is also when I plant the first of the year's seeds. Right now I have two types of chilli, Padrón and Cayenne, in a propagator under my desk. I also have a couple of trays of peas, and one of broad beans. Here they will benefit from the floor-length window as they germinate into life. There are no shoots yet but I check them every day, just in case. One morning they will surprise and delight me. Outside the overwintering edible

March

Pastéis de Belém
Smoked salmon & chive soufflé
Rhubarb & rosewater pavlova
Omelette with Caerphilly
& wild garlic
Mocha éclairs
Herby French toast with sun-blush
tomatoes, avocado & crispy bacon
Chinese egg & prawn custard, with
stir-fried greens and rice
Sticky toffee pudding
Purple sprouting broccoli with
lemony hollandaise

April

Wild garlic, spinach & pecorino
gnocchi with tomato sauce
Classic hot cross buns
Rhubarb & custard tart
Pasta 'carbonara' with cavolo nero
Béarnaise sauce
Apricot and hazelnut roulade
Watercress & brie flamiche
Crispy bacon, asparagus & egg salad
with creamy mustard dressing
Stem ginger, raisin & whisky steamed
pudding

May

Coffee & walnut cake
Crab & egg 'brik'
Huevos revueltos with asparagus
& prawns
Fig & oloroso upside-down cake
Stir-fried vegetable noodles with chilli
egg and soy salmon
Greek lemon, egg & asparagus soup
Indian spiced potato pancakes with
coriander & tomato chutney
Bacon & fried egg sarnie

plants are also making good progress now the days are lengthening. I notice the first dark buds appearing on the stems of the purple sprouting broccoli, indicating that soon, at last, there will be something to harvest. I planted plenty, taking a some-for-us, some-for-the-chickens approach to my sowing. Under its terracotta forcing pot, the rhubarb plant is slowly coming out of winter dormancy, its tight pink buds unfurling into crunched-up crinkly leaves. The bare branches of the grapevine show the merest of swellings just under the surface. Happily it won't be long before it too surges back into life.

The chickens sense change too. They seem more active, and are very perky and vocal when I go into the garden. Finally I take off the wooden boards that shelter half of their run from the worst of the winter weather, instantly giving them more air and sunlight, like opening up the shutters on a dusty room. Sadly for them, they cannot yet free-range in the garden. The tender and tasty shoots emerging all over the place would be devoured in seconds if I let the hens roam unwatched, and the garden would be finished before it had even got going. To compensate, I give the chickens extra treats. Deeply ferrous leaves from the cavolo nero, slightly past-it bananas and stale cake are all great favourites. Once the young plants are more established, the hens will be allowed some time to forage by themselves.

Spring's recipes are about revitalizing and lifting the mood.

3rd March

Pastéis de Belém – warm Portuguese custard tarts

I first tasted *pastéis de Belém* on holiday in Lisbon when I was a child, and so exquisite were they that I have not forgotten the taste nearly three decades later. Many, if not most, of my pleasurable memories centre around food. Lucky for me then that my mum, a single parent, worked exceptionally hard to take us on a foreign holiday as often as she could afford, opening our eyes wide to a wonderful edible world out there. For this I will always be grateful.

I distinctly remember the café in which we ate the tarts: sombre waiters in stiff black and white uniforms, walls covered in blue-and-white-patterned ceramic tiles, the whirring ceiling fans and the hiss of the espresso machine, and most of all the tarts themselves. Crisp, flaky pastry filled to the brim with wobbly, vanilla-scented custard, the finishing touches a dusting of cinnamon and a caramelized top. So much more of a treat than our own English custard tarts, which were soggy and stodgy by comparison.

Now with such a plentiful supply of eggs I have no excuse not to make them myself. They are pretty straightforward, but you'll need nerves of steel and an exceptionally hot oven to get the all-important caramelization. They are best eaten within a few hours of being made – they are so delicious this shouldn't pose a problem.

Makes 12

300ml milk

1 vanilla pod, split lengthways

175g caster sugar

25g plain flour, plus extra for dusting

3 egg yolks

1 whole egg

375g pack of ready-rolled puff pastry (use half and save the rest)

1 heaped tsp ground cinnamon

Vegetable oil for greasing

Make the custard filling: pour the milk into a small saucepan, add the vanilla pod and bring gently up to just below boiling point. Turn off the heat and set the milk aside to infuse for 15 minutes.

Put the sugar in a large bowl and sift over the flour, mixing together well, then beat in the egg yolks and whole egg until you have a thick creamy paste. Remove the vanilla pod from the milk, scraping in the seeds as you go, and discard the pod. Pour the vanilla-scented milk into the bowl and beat together until really well mixed. The custard requires no further cooking now, and needs to go completely cold so it doesn't overcook when it bakes.

Cut the roll of pastry in half through the middle, saving one half for another recipe. Unroll it, evenly sprinkle over the cinnamon, then reroll tightly. Wrap in clingfilm and chill in the freezer for 20 minutes.

When the custard is cold and the pastry chilled and firm, turn on your oven to its highest setting – mine goes to 240°C – and let it get up to temperature. Brush the insides of a 12-hole muffin tray with a little vegetable oil. Cut the roll of pastry into twelve 5–7mm-thick discs. Take each disc and flatten it on a lightly floured worktop using the palm of your hand. The aim is to get the pastry as thin as you can without creating any holes. Use the flattened discs to line the muffin tin. Pour the cold custard evenly into each, taking care not to spill any over the edges – I find a jug the easiest way of doing this.

Very quickly open the oven, set the tray on the highest shelf and close it again. The oven will be fiercely hot and it's important not to lose the heat. Cook the tarts for 10–12 minutes, by which time the pastry will be crisp and the surface of the tarts speckled with deep dark patches. Be brave – you are treading a fine line between caramelized custard and burnt pastry.

Remove from the oven and allow to cool to room temperature.

6th March

Smoked salmon & chive soufflé

INDULGENT SUPPER FOR ONE

I would hate to give the impression that I regularly cook soufflés on a weeknight, especially just for myself. My cooking normally resides rather more squarely in the real world than that. But I was home alone, and I can't deny that this is exactly what I did. I had a bit of leftover smoked salmon in the fridge that sorely needed a good home, and I fancied trying something new. The kids had gone to bed, the menagerie had been fed and the house was blissfully, finally, quiet. This time of day is my favourite time to cook, just me and a glass of wine as I potter, taste, chop and stir. No one to please but myself, and what could be more relaxing than that?

Serves 1, or 2 as a starter

25g unsalted butter

20g flour

150ml milk

2 tbsp mascarpone or full-fat cream cheese

1 egg, separated

1 tbsp finely chopped chives

50g smoked salmon, chopped, plus a little extra to garnish

Salt & freshly ground black pepper

Preheat the oven to 180°C/Gas 4. You will need 2 small ramekins or 1 individual, straight-sided pie dish.

Melt the butter in a saucepan over a low heat. Brush a little melted butter inside the ramekins or pie dish, and add the flour to the rest in the pan. Stir to form a roux, which will look a little like wet sand. Pour in the milk and whisk until you have a thick, smooth, white sauce. Turn off the heat. Stir through the mascarpone or cream cheese, followed by the egg yolk, chives and salmon, stirring well to mix evenly. Season generously.

In a clean bowl, whisk the egg white until stiff. Using a metal spoon, fold the egg white through the soufflé mixture in a figure-of-eight motion. Take care not to over-mix or you will knock valuable air out. Pour into the prepared ramekins or dish and bake in the oven for 20–25 minutes for smaller soufflés, or 25–30 minutes for a larger one.

Garnish with a few extra strips of smoked salmon and eat immediately.

10th March

Rhubarb & rosewater pavlova

A PRETTY, PALE PINK PUDDING FOR EARLY SPRING

I love rhubarb so much I have just planted a second clump in the garden, this time a 'Champagne' variety known for its vibrant pink stems. Unfortunately it won't be ready to harvest for at least a year, and my original plant has not yet grown enough for me to pull out any stems, so I have to be content to buy rhubarb for a little while longer.

This pudding was unashamedly feminine, the thin, pale pink stems enhanced to another level of 'girlishness' by the addition of rosewater. That's not to say the men didn't enjoy eating it as much as we did. Meringue, cream and fruit seem to have been invented for each other. As a final flourish I drizzle a little extra honey over the pavlova, not for extra sweetness, but because it makes it even prettier.

I make meringues in my trusty food mixer, but an electric whisk in a large bowl would do the job just as well. I wouldn't, however, contemplate making them by hand – it sounds to me like too much work.

Enough for about 6, depending on greed

For the meringue:

3 egg whites

200g caster sugar (or double the weight of the egg whites)

1 tbsp rosewater

For the filling:

400g young pink rhubarb stems, cut into 4–5cm lengths

50g caster sugar

300ml double cream

2 tbsp runny honey, plus a little for drizzling

4 tbsp full-fat Greek yogurt

1–2 tbsp rosewater

Preheat the oven to 100°C/Gas ¼. Line a baking tray with baking paper.

Tip the egg whites into the very clean bowl of a food mixer and whisk until stiff. Add about a third of the sugar and whisk until completely combined, then add a third more and whisk again. Add the final third and whisk on high for 2 minutes. Pour in the rosewater and whisk once more for a further minute to ensure it is thoroughly mixed. Scrape the meringue into a pile in the centre of the baking tray and use a spatula to spread out to a circle of about 23–24cm diameter. Hollow out the centre a little so the sides stand a couple of centimetres higher. Bake for 2½ hours, after which it should lift cleanly off the baking paper. If it doesn't, return to the oven for another few minutes. Remove and allow to cool completely, then transfer to a serving plate.

Lay the rhubarb in a single layer in a shallow pan – I used a deep frying pan. Add a little water, just 2 tablespoons or so, and sprinkle over the sugar. Set over a medium heat, cover tightly with a lid or foil, and poach for 10 minutes. Turn off the heat and allow to cool.

Whisk the cream with the honey in a large bowl until lightly whipped but not too stiff. Fold through the yogurt and stir in rosewater to taste. Then, using a large metal spoon, lightly fold in half the rhubarb, along with a little of the syrup. Don't mix too thoroughly: you want to marble the fruit through the cream.

Spoon into the centre of the cool meringue and level out with the flat of a knife. Spread the rest of the rhubarb evenly over the top and trickle over any remaining poaching syrup. Finally drizzle over a little extra honey, allowing it to spill over the sides of the meringue and on to the plate.

14th March

Omelette with Caerphilly & wild garlic

Wild garlic is now forming a lush green carpet in the woods at the bottom of our hill. The season is brief, just a few weeks from early March, and I try to gather it as often as possible. If I'm feeling time-rich or I just can't resist the lure of the morning sun, I walk the dogs the long way home after the school run, the exercise and fresh air doing us all the world of good. Today's longer walk saw the extra benefit of a bag of wild garlic leaves and a hastily concocted plan to use them in an omelette for lunch.

I do think an omelette is perfect for one and if I am working at home it is often on my lunch menu. Simple and speedy, this one was on the table in three minutes flat, much faster than I could make a decent sarnie. The garlic was so fresh and delicious, it didn't take me much longer than that to eat it, meaning I was soon back at my desk and making up for time lost dithering about with the dogs in the morning.

If you can't get hold of wild garlic, you could make this with a handful of spinach leaves wilted with a little crushed garlic. But the real thing is worth hunting down and not as uncommon as you

might think. We live but a mile from the city centre, where a thin ribbon of woodland follows a brook downstream. If you have even a small patch of woods near you, go exploring. You never know, you might be lucky. The vibrant green, strap-like leaves are unmissable by their scent alone.

Enough for one

A knob of butter, about 10g

A generous handful of wild garlic leaves, about 40g, thoroughly washed & roughly chopped

Salt & freshly ground black pepper

A splash of olive oil

2 eggs, lightly beaten

50g Caerphilly or other crumbly cheese (like Cheshire or Wensleydale), broken up

Melt the butter in a small frying pan and as it starts to foam, toss in the wild garlic and stir-fry for a minute until it just wilts, seasoning with a little salt and pepper. Tip on to a plate and add a splash of olive oil to the pan, allowing it to get hot over a medium-high flame.

    Lightly beat the eggs in a small bowl; season. When the oil is hot, pour in the egg. Using a fork, draw the sides in as the omelette cooks and tip the pan from side to side to spread the egg out. When it is almost set, scatter over the cheese and the wilted wild garlic. Fold in half, slide on to a plate and eat immediately.

16th March

Mocha éclairs

FOR A FRIDAY TREAT

I always like to have a treat on a Friday night – after a long working week it's good to have something nice as a reward. So after school I enlist the help of the kids and we do a bit of baking. More often than not they get waylaid by the TV, the computer or their bikes, leaving me to do most of the work. Funnily enough, they normally reappear at that critical bowl-licking stage …

Éclairs have always been a favourite of mine, the coffee ones in particular, as they are decadent without being too sickly sweet. They are not tricky to make. A piping bag will give you the classic shape, but don't be put off if you don't have one, because a sandwich bag with the corner snipped off will suffice. Or go freeform and spoon them into mounds like large profiteroles.

Makes about 8 éclairs

60g strong plain flour (bread flour)

1 tsp caster sugar

150ml cold water

50g butter, cut into small cubes

2 eggs

For the mocha icing:

60g dark chocolate

3 tbsp very strong black coffee (espresso strength)

150g icing sugar, sieved

For the filling:

300ml double cream

1 tbsp very strong black coffee (espresso strength)

2 heaped tsp icing sugar

Preheat the oven to 200°C/Gas 6.

Sift the flour into a bowl, sprinkle over the caster sugar and leave ready by the hob. Measure the water into a saucepan and add the butter. Set over a medium heat and bring up to a boil. As soon as the butter has melted and the water is bubbling, turn off the heat and tip in the flour in one go, stirring as you do so. Keep stirring and after 30 seconds or so, the mixture should have come together as a smooth paste. Set aside to cool for 10 minutes.

Prepare two baking trays by cutting baking paper to fit. Run the paper under the cold tap then shake off the excess water. The wet paper will create a steamy atmosphere that helps the éclairs to rise in the oven.

Crack the eggs into a jug and beat together lightly. Add the egg, a little at a time, to the cooled flour paste, beating thoroughly between each addition. After all the egg has been incorporated, you will have a smooth glossy paste. Spoon into a piping bag fitted with a 1cm smooth-sided nozzle – or use a plastic sandwich bag with the corner cut off – and pipe 4 éclairs, roughly 10cm long, on to each sheet. Bake in the hot oven for 20 minutes. Remove from the oven and, using a small knife, pierce a hole in each end of the éclairs, then return them to the trays upside down. This allows steam to escape, helping them crisp up. Bake for a further 10 minutes until they are crisp and a deep golden brown. Remove and allow to cool completely on a wire rack.

Make the icing by melting the chocolate in a bowl, either over a pan of barely simmering water or in a microwave on high for a minute and a half. Stir the coffee through then sift over the icing sugar, beating to a smooth paste. If it is a little dry, add a splash more coffee or water.

Prepare the filling by whisking together the cream, coffee and icing sugar in a roomy bowl, taking care not to over-beat. Spoon the cream into a piping bag, cut a slit down the side of each éclair and pipe the coffee cream inside. Then spread over a layer of icing. Put to one side for the icing to set, about 30 minutes, before tucking in.

Herby French toast with sun-blush tomatoes, avocado & crispy bacon

More commonly eaten as a sweet brunch dish drizzled with maple syrup, French toast also makes a tasty and speedy supper for times when you can't be fussed to make a proper sit-down meal. In this version the bread was soaked in eggs flavoured with dried herbs and a shake of Tabasco. There is some snobbery around dried herbs but they certainly have a place in my kitchen. The more robust woody varieties, such as thyme and oregano, retain their aromas well.

Serves 2

For the dressing:

1 tsp wholegrain mustard

2 tbsp extra virgin olive oil

1 tsp white wine vinegar

A pinch of caster sugar

Salt & freshly ground black pepper

For the French toast:

3 eggs

75ml single cream

1 heaped tsp dried mixed herbs

A dash of chilli sauce, such as Tabasco (optional)

Salt & freshly ground black pepper

2 slices thick-cut white bread

A knob of butter

6 slices streaky bacon

A generous handful of rocket

1 large ripe avocado, sliced

100g sun-blush tomatoes

First, make the dressing by whisking all the ingredients together in a small bowl. Set aside.

Then, in another small bowl, whisk together the eggs and the cream, with the herbs, chilli sauce and a generous seasoning of salt and pepper. Lay the bread in a single layer in a shallow dish and pour over the egg mixture. Set aside for 3 minutes for the bread to soak up the custard, then carefully turn over the slices and leave for another couple of minutes, by which time the custard should have all been absorbed. If it hasn't quite got there, leave it a little longer.

While the bread is soaking, melt the butter in a large frying pan and fry the bacon until crisp on both sides. Remove and drain on kitchen paper, keeping warm by covering loosely with another sheet of paper.

With the heat on medium-high, fry the slices of bread for about 2 minutes on each side until crisp and golden. Remove and top each slice with a little rocket, the bacon, avocado and sun-blush tomatoes. Drizzle over the dressing and eat immediately.

24th March

Chinese egg & prawn custard, with stir-fried greens and rice

This dish took me out of my cooking comfort zone. I had come across a sort of savoury egg custard in my well-thumbed copy of Madhur Jaffrey's excellent book *Far Eastern Cookery*, and I had long wanted to try my own version of it. While I am fairly confident when it comes to South-east Asian cooking, Chinese food is not so familiar – we never ate it as kids and I have never travelled there. But my fear of the unknown proved to be unfounded, and I wished I had tried it sooner. The method is simple and the dish very rewarding, almost like a light version of an omelette with lots of tasty bits in it.

We ate the eggs alongside some stir-fried greens from the garden, tossed in garlic slivers and ginger, and a dish of fluffy white rice. I

have a method of cooking rice that is so failsafe I feel I must pass it on. I am mostly self-taught when it comes to cooking, but many years ago I went on a month-long residential cookery course run by a lovely lady called Rosie Davies. Rosie passed on to me her way of cooking rice, and I have followed it faithfully ever since. It works with any quantity of rice – what is important is the level of water you cover it with.

Serves 4

250g basmati rice

30g dried shiitake mushrooms

8 eggs

4 spring onions, finely chopped

1 clove garlic, crushed

3 tbsp toasted sesame oil

3 tbsp light soy sauce

1 tsp caster sugar

Salt & white pepper

200g cooked prawns

1 tbsp vegetable oil

For the greens:

1 tbsp vegetable oil

2 cloves garlic, finely sliced

2cm fresh ginger, peeled & finely sliced

350g spring greens, washed and sliced

3 tsp light soy sauce

3 tsp toasted sesame oil

3 tsp rice wine vinegar

Wash the rice under plenty of running water and leave to soak for 30 minutes in cold water.

Put the dried mushrooms in a small bowl, cover with boiling water and leave to soak for 30 minutes. Drain, reserving 4 tablespoons of soaking water, and chop finely. Add to a bowl, along with the reserved water. Crack in the eggs and beat together. Add the spring onions, garlic, sesame oil, soy sauce and caster sugar and mix thoroughly. Season generously with salt and white pepper.

Divide the prawns between 4 large ramekins – mine were 10cm across, 5cm deep – then pour over the egg mixture. Set a bamboo steamer over a wok of boiling water and carefully lower the dishes in. Steam, covered, for about 12–15 minutes, or until a skewer inserted into the centre comes out clean – topping up the steamer water if necessary.

Once the eggs have started to cook, drain the rice, shaking off as much water as possible. Add a tablespoon of vegetable oil to a saucepan and set over a medium heat. When hot, tip in the rice and toss to coat in the oil. Pour over boiling water until it comes to just a centimetre above the rice, and stir once to separate the grains. Clamp on a tight-fitting lid and boil for exactly 1 minute. Turn off the heat and leave completely undisturbed for 12 minutes, then remove the lid and fluff up with a fork.

When the eggs are cooked, remove the steamer to a plate to rest while you cook the greens. Pour the water from the wok, dry and return to the heat. Add the vegetable oil, garlic and ginger and stir-fry for a minute until turning golden. Tip in the greens and add the soy, sesame oil and rice wine vinegar. Stir-fry for a couple of minutes until the greens are just tender.

Serve each egg custard alongside a mound of rice topped with the greens.

25th March

Sticky toffee pudding

IN THE GARDEN

Sticky toffee pudding is probably the ultimate Sunday lunch dessert, one that everyone seems to love. We had friends coming over and I had long since hatched a plan to make it. Spring in this country seems to lurch crazily and unpredictably from cold one day to hot the next, and my cooking tries to follow suit. Today turned out to be unseasonably warm and we ended up lighting the BBQ, dressed in shorts and T-shirts, and eating in the garden in the hot sunshine – the first al fresco lunch of the year. But the sticky toffee pudding stayed on the menu, and funnily enough there was not one complaint.

Serves 6, generously

200g dried dates, roughly chopped

175ml boiling water

1 tsp vanilla extract

125g butter, at room temperature

75g dark brown sugar

2 tbsp black treacle

3 eggs

250g self-raising flour

1 tsp bicarbonate of soda

A pinch of salt

For the sauce:

150g dark brown sugar

2 tbsp black treacle

150ml cold water

75g butter, cut into cubes

100ml double cream

1 tsp vanilla extract

Put the dates in a small bowl and pour the boiling water over. Stir through the vanilla extract and set aside to soak for 30 minutes.

Preheat the oven to 180°C/Gas 4.

Tip the softened dates and any residual soaking water into a food processor and whizz to a purée. Add the butter, sugar and treacle and process again until thoroughly combined. Crack in the eggs, one at a time, mixing between each addition. Finally add the flour, bicarbonate of soda and salt and process to a smooth batter. Scrape into a baking dish and cook for about 45 minutes or until a skewer inserted into the centre comes out clean. Cover the top loosely with foil if it is getting too dark.

While the cake is baking, prepare the sauce. Put the sugar and treacle in a heavy-based pan and pour in the water. Bring to the boil and simmer for a minute or so, stirring until all the sugar has dissolved. Add the butter, cream and vanilla, and simmer until melted, stirring well to give a nice glossy sauce.

When the pudding is cooked, remove it from the oven and prick all over with a skewer. Slowly pour over about half the toffee sauce, allowing it to soak into the sponge. Serve the rest of the sauce in a jug for people to help themselves, along with some cream or ice cream.

27th March
Purple sprouting broccoli with lemony hollandaise

An exciting day in my gardening year: finally, months and months after planting the seeds, my purple sprouting broccoli is ready for harvesting. It is the first year I have managed to grow it to maturity – previous years' crops having been subject to death-by-mollusc in the seedling stage – and it has been most satisfying watching it develop. The mature plants are handsome, bushy things, and for the last couple of weeks I have been trimming off the largest leaves to let more light at the developing shoots. The chickens get very animated when they see me, and pace up and down their run clucking excitedly, knowing they will be the recipients of the leafy offcuts.

Hollandaise sauce is one of those things that can send shivers of fear down the spine of even the most competent of cooks, myself included. But, like most things, regular practice brings confidence, and with confidence the fear evaporates. The most important thing to remember is not to allow the sauce to get too hot or it will separate. I remove the bowl from the heat source at regular intervals, resting it on a cool work surface as I continue whisking for a few seconds to reduce the temperature, and I never, ever, let the bowl actually touch the water in the saucepan. We ate this with some grilled chicken thighs.

Serves 2, as a side dish or starter

2 egg yolks

Juice & finely grated zest of 1 lemon

Salt & freshly ground black pepper

100g butter, melted

2–3 generous handfuls purple sprouting broccoli (about 200g)

Pour a little water, just a couple of centimetres or so, into a heavy-based saucepan, set over a low heat and bring up to a gentle simmer.

Place the egg yolks in a large, preferably non-metallic, heatproof bowl. A metal bowl will get very hot very quickly, increasing the chance of the sauce overheating. A thick heatproof glass bowl is ideal. Whisk in half the lemon juice and the lemon zest, and season with a little salt and pepper. Rest the bowl over the saucepan of water and whisk for a couple of minutes over a very low heat until it starts to thicken a little. Then begin to add the melted butter, a teaspoon at a time at first, increasing to a thin trickle after the first few additions, whisking continuously. Remove the bowl from the pan and rest on the work surface every now and then as you whisk to cool the sauce a little, before returning to the heat. Once all the butter has been whisked in, you should have a sauce the consistency of mayonnaise. Taste to check the seasoning, adding a splash more lemon juice if it needs sharpening a little. Remove the pan from the heat and set aside to keep warm while you cook the broccoli.

Bring a large pan of salted water to a rolling boil and plunge in the purple sprouting broccoli. Cook for 3 minutes until it is tender but with a little bite. Drain thoroughly and arrange on a warm serving plate. Spoon over the hollandaise and serve immediately.

Wild garlic, spinach & pecorino gnocchi with tomato sauce

Today a walk through the woods yielded a big bag of wild garlic for us and a big bag for the chickens. Knowing their love for green stuff I thought it would make a nice treat for them, but they seem a little unimpressed so far. Never mind.

The wild garlic season is so brief I make something with it a couple of times a week to get my fill. You can use it in place of spinach in any recipe, and in my kitchen it often finds its way into salads, risottos and soups. Or chop it up very fine and mash through some butter for a vivid green spread to melt over new potatoes or toast. If you cannot get hold of wild garlic, use an equal weight of spinach and stir through a crushed clove of garlic.

I find potato-based gnocchi a bit heavy-going. I prefer to make them with ricotta, which gives them a more delicate texture. To keep them as light and airy as possible, don't over-mix or over-handle them. They do take a little while to roll, but once made will keep in the fridge for several hours, so make them when you have time.

A hearty supper for 2

200g wild garlic leaves

200g spinach

250g ricotta cheese

50g pecorino cheese, finely grated, plus a little extra to serve

2 eggs

100g plain flour, plus extra for dusting

Salt & freshly ground black pepper

For the tomato sauce:

2 tbsp olive oil

1 large onion, finely chopped

1 clove garlic, crushed

1 x 400g tin chopped plum tomatoes

1 tsp caster sugar

Salt & freshly ground black pepper

Wash the wild garlic and spinach thoroughly and shake off most of the water. Then pack it into a large pan with a tight-fitting lid and set over a medium heat. Cook for 4–5 minutes until it has completely wilted down, turning it halfway through to make sure it wilts evenly. Drain well, allow to cool for a few minutes, then squeeze out as much water as possible, tip on to a chopping board and chop finely.

In a large bowl mix together the ricotta, pecorino, eggs and flour, seasoning well with salt and black pepper. Add the chopped spinach and wild garlic and fold through until just combined. Chill in the fridge for 30 minutes so the mixture stiffens a little and becomes easier to shape.

Sprinkle a light dusting of flour on to a baking tray and over your hands, and make the gnocchi by gently forming a generous teaspoon of the mixture into a little ball in your palm. Lay it on the baking tray and repeat. Your hands will no doubt get sticky – when they do, stop, wash and dry them, and start again, otherwise you will get into a mess. Cover the gnocchi loosely with clingfilm and refrigerate until you are ready to eat.

Make the tomato sauce by heating the oil in a frying pan and gently sweating the onion for around 10–15 minutes until it is soft and translucent. Add the garlic and fry for a further minute before pouring in the tomatoes and half a tin of cold water. Stir through the sugar and season with a little salt and black pepper. Simmer steadily for around 20 minutes until thick and rich.

When ready to eat, bring a large pan of salted water up to the boil then lower the heat to a gentle simmer. Carefully add half the gnocchi and poach them for 4–5 minutes until they float to the surface. Remove to a plate with a slotted spoon and cover loosely in foil to keep warm. Repeat with the remaining gnocchi.

To serve, preheat the grill. Pour the hot tomato sauce into a baking dish and scatter over the gnocchi. Grate over a little extra pecorino and flash under a hot grill for a couple of minutes until the cheese is golden. Serve immediately.

6th April

Classic hot cross buns

COMFORT BAKING

Why go to the bother of making your own hot cross buns? Well, first, you can add as much spice as you like, and secondly your house will smell divine as they bake. This recipe, like a lot of breads – particularly the sweet ones, uses an egg to enrich and soften the dough. The flour-paste cross on the top adds nothing in the taste department but is completely necessary all the same.

Makes 12 buns

150ml hand-hot water (use half boiling & half cold)

1 tbsp dried yeast

40g caster sugar

500g strong (bread) flour

1 heaped tsp ground mixed spice

1 tsp salt

50g butter, melted

1 beaten egg

75ml warm milk

Vegetable oil for greasing

75g raisins or currants

50g chopped mixed peel

For the topping:

4 tbsp plain flour

4 tbsp cold water

2 tbsp caster sugar

2 tbsp boiling water

Measure the water into a jug, stir through the yeast and a teaspoon of the caster sugar. Set aside for about 10 minutes until a foamy head forms on the surface.

Sift the flour into a large mixing bowl and stir through the spice, salt and the rest of the caster sugar. Make a well in the middle and set aside.

In another mixing jug or small bowl, beat together the melted butter, egg and warm milk. Pour into the well in the flour, along with the foaming yeast. Mix together with a spoon until the

dough comes together in a rough ball, then tip on to the work surface. Knead the dough for at least 5 minutes, pushing away with the heel of your hand and rolling back towards you until it becomes stretchy and smooth. If it is sticking to the worktop, add a little flour, but be careful not to add too much or it will become dry. The fluffiest lightest bread comes from dough that is a bit sticky and wet to work with.

Place the dough in a bowl which you have lightly oiled, and cover with a clean tea towel or piece of clingfilm. Set aside in a warm place until the dough has doubled in size. Depending on the temperature of the room, this will take an hour or two, maybe longer.

Once the dough has doubled in size, tip on to the worktop and flatten slightly with the palm of your hand. Sprinkle over the dried fruit and mixed peel and gently knead into the dough. Using a knife, cut the dough in half, then cut each half into 6 equal-sized pieces. Gently roll each piece into a ball, tucking any fruit under the surface as much as possible because it can burn in the oven, and place in a deep-sided baking tin lined with baking paper. (You need a deep tin so that when you cover it, the buns have room to rise without sticking to the clingfilm.) Repeat with the remaining dough until you have 12 buns equally spaced in the baking tin. Cover lightly with a double layer of clingfilm, tucking it under the tray to keep the air out. Leave to prove again for 30–45 minutes until the buns have risen by half.

Preheat the oven to 220°C/Gas 7.

Once the buns have proved for the final time, prepare the flour paste for the 'crosses' by mixing the flour and cold water until smooth. Spoon into a small sandwich bag and snip off a tiny corner to create a quick piping bag. Pipe crosses on to each bun. Transfer to the hot oven and bake for about 10 minutes until golden brown. While they are cooking, dissolve the caster sugar in the boiling water. As soon as you remove the buns from the oven, glaze them by brushing with the sugar syrup. Put them on a rack to cool.

14th April

Rhubarb & custard tart

FOR A GARDEN FEAST

Today felt like mid-summer rather than mid-spring, a light breeze and gorgeous sunshine all day. My friend Jo came over, with a nice bottle of rosé, and we happily cooked and gossiped the afternoon away in the kitchen as we watched our kids charge about the garden. We were cooking up a feast for an early evening family BBQ: meaty pork ribs marinated with ginger and soy, a coriander and chilli sauce to be poured over a side of crisp grilled salmon, and a wobbly custard tart studded with pieces of sharp rhubarb from the garden to finish. The inspiration for this was the 'rhubarb and custard' boiled sweets I loved so much as a child, the sharp, almost fizzy, rhubarb side contrasting with the smooth, creamy, custard side – sweet shop perfection. I caramelized the surface of the tart with a little Demerara sugar, which made it look pretty and added a lovely 'crunch', but it would be just as good without if you felt this was a step too far.

Out of convenience I usually use my food processor to make pastry, and I think it is possible to make it just as deliciously light and crumbly as by the old-fashioned, hand-rubbed method.

Makes 6 generous slices

300g rhubarb, in 4–5cm slices
80g granulated sugar

For the pastry:
200g plain flour, plus extra for dusting
125g cold butter, cubed
2 tbsp icing sugar
2 tbsp icy cold water

For the custard:
300ml single cream
1 vanilla pod, split lengthways
4 egg yolks
50g caster sugar
1–2 tbsp Demerara sugar, to finish (optional)

You will need a 25cm loose-based metal flan tin, baking paper and baking beans for this.

Put the rhubarb in a single layer in a wide saucepan – a deep frying pan is ideal. Sprinkle over the sugar, add a mere tablespoon or two of cold water and cover with a lid or foil. Poach over a low heat for around 10 minutes until soft when pierced with the tip of a sharp knife. Resist the urge to stir – you don't want the pieces to break up – but give the pan a gentle shake from time to time so the rhubarb doesn't stick. Set aside to cool.

To make the pastry, put the flour and butter in a food processor and pulse a few brief times until it resembles rough breadcrumbs. Add the icing sugar and pulse once more. Add the water and pulse until it just starts to come together. Tip on to a sheet of clingfilm, press together into a ball, wrap up tightly and chill in the fridge for 30 minutes.

While the pastry is chilling, pour the cream into a small pan and add the vanilla pod. Warm the cream, taking care not to let it boil or it may split, then turn off the heat and leave to infuse.

Preheat the oven to 180°C/Gas 4. Roll out the pastry on a lightly floured surface, then gently lift it into the tin, pressing it right down into the bottom. To trim, roll the rolling pin quickly over the top of the tin, chopping off the overhanging pastry. Line with paper and beans and bake blind for 15–20 minutes until golden and crisp on the edges. Remove the beans and paper and bake for 5 more minutes until cooked through. Take out of the oven and allow to cool a little, then spread over the cooled rhubarb and any syrup.

To finish the custard, fish out the vanilla pod, scraping the seeds into the custard as you do so. Add the egg yolks and sugar and mix thoroughly, then pour on top of the rhubarb. Carefully transfer to the oven – sliding it on to a baking tray helps prevent slops – and bake for 20 minutes, or until the custard has just set. Remove and cool to room temperature before eating.

To caramelize the surface, sprinkle over a little Demerara sugar and flash it quickly under a hot grill, or blast it with a blow torch if you have one.

16th April

Pasta 'carbonara' with cavolo nero

Before you read any further, I warn you this recipe is inauthentic in the extreme. Generations of Italian Mammas will be turning in their graves at my impertinence in calling this a carbonara. But this is the sort of easy pasta dish I make almost weekly throughout the year: an onion cooked down to an intensely sweet base, a little bacon (or even some smoked salmon), a handful of veggies, a drizzle of cream and a couple of eggs to thicken and enrich. It *is* a sort of carbonara.

Today's incarnation had very thin ribbons of deep green cavolo nero twirling through the spaghetti. The handful of plants I have been nurturing in the garden for months and months have finally matured and we are enjoying the harvest several times a week.

Serves 2 for a generous and comforting supper

120g smoked streaky bacon, chopped

1 tbsp olive oil, plus an extra drizzle

1 large onion, finely chopped

200g dried spaghetti

2 generous handfuls of cavolo nero (or other dark green leaves), about 120g, washed and shredded into spaghetti-thin ribbons

2 cloves garlic, crushed

100ml Marsala

3 tbsp crème fraîche

2 eggs

40g freshly grated Parmesan

Salt & freshly ground black pepper

In a wide, deep frying pan, toss the bacon in the oil and fry over a medium heat for 10 minutes or so until it is starting to crisp and colour at the edges. Reduce the heat to as low as possible, add the onion and sweat until it is soft and almost melting. The sweetness you get from the long, slow cooking of onions cannot be beaten, so don't try to rush this step: it will take at least 20 minutes, if

not 30, to do it properly. A sheet of damp baking paper over the surface will create a steamy lid that helps the process along.

While the onions are cooking, bring a generous pan of salted water up to a vigorous boil and cook the pasta until *al dente*. A minute before it is due to be ready, add the shredded cavolo nero and stir to push it under the water. Cook for a mere minute so that it retains a little crunch, then drain the pasta and cavolo nero well, tossing in a drizzle of olive oil. Set aside while you finish the sauce.

When the onions are really soft, turn the heat back up again and add the garlic, frying for just a minute or so until you can smell the aroma wafting up from the pan. Then pour in the Marsala and allow it to bubble away and evaporate. Add the crème fraîche, eggs and most of the Parmesan, reserving a little for sprinkling on top. Season to taste, being generous with the black pepper. Stir thoroughly to mix, then tip in the pasta and cavolo nero, tossing together for a couple of minutes until everything is really hot. Serve in warmed bowls, with the rest of the Parmesan scattered over the top.

20th April

Béarnaise sauce

FOR A STEAK & CHIP SUPPER

Most foods have a seasonal feel to them – it feels right to eat a stew in autumn and a quiche in summer – and this is the way I love to eat, allowing my body and the weather to jog along in happy harmony. But some things I can tuck into at any time of year. A thick juicy steak is just as satisfying to eat when seared on the barbecue in the heat of the summer sun as it is to devour on a cold evening in winter. Steak is a weekend treat, whatever the weather.

Ribeye is my cut of choice, having just the right balance between flavour and tenderness, and for preference I share one big fat steak between two. A thick-cut steak is easier to cook just how I like it, which is rare but by no means blue, with a crisp caramelized outside. I then slice it thinly across the grain into tender ribbons and serve it with plenty of chips and soft old-fashioned English lettuce, and some sort of sauce to dunk it all in. Sometimes this is a simple dollop of mayo from a jar, perhaps enlivened with a clove of crushed garlic, but tonight I was feeling generous and made a rich Béarnaise to cheer us up on a wild, wet and windy spring evening.

Béarnaise sauce is essentially a herby version of hollandaise, in which the lemon juice has been replaced by a concentrated vinegar and shallot reduction. I normally add a little crushed garlic, too, as for me steak and chips would not be quite right without the pungency it brings. Béarnaise is classically partnered with steak, but is also great with plain grilled salmon or sliced roast chicken. Like hollandaise, some care needs to be taken to ensure the emulsion doesn't overheat and split as you are whisking, but otherwise it is straightforward to make.

For 2, served alongside steak, chips and salad

4 tbsp white wine vinegar

1 shallot, finely chopped

1 clove garlic, chopped

3 sprigs of fresh tarragon, plus 2 tbsp chopped fresh leaves

A few black peppercorns

2 egg yolks

100g unsalted butter, cut into 1cm cubes and softened to room temperature

Salt & freshly ground black pepper

Place the vinegar, shallot, garlic, tarragon sprigs and peppercorns in a small saucepan. Bring up to the boil and simmer gently for a few minutes until it has reduced to about a tablespoon of liquid. Strain into a small bowl, then wash the pan and add a couple of centimetres of water. Set over a low heat.

Put the egg yolks into a heatproof bowl with a couple of the cubes of butter and set over the saucepan, making sure the base of the bowl is well away from the water. A thick glass bowl is preferable to a metal one as it heats more slowly and evenly. Using a balloon whisk, mix together over a low heat until the egg starts to thicken a little. Pour in the vinegar reduction and whisk together. Now begin to add the rest of the butter, a couple of pieces at a time, whisking as it melts into the sauce. To stop the sauce getting too hot, raise the bowl off the heat from time to time, allowing it to cool for 30 seconds or so on the worktop, while you keep on whisking. Keep adding the butter and whisking until you are left with a glossy smooth sauce the consistency of double cream. Stir through the chopped tarragon and taste to check the seasoning, adding a little salt and black pepper. Turn off the heat and leave the bowl set over the pan to keep warm until you are ready to use it.

21st April

Apricot and hazelnut roulade

A RETRO PUDDING

One of my first jobs was working as the Saturday girl in a cake shop and café, when I was about twelve. It was here that I first came across the amazing confection called a 'roulade', a soft airy sponge rolled around billowing whipped cream studded with fruit, sometimes strawberries, sometimes apricots. It was unlike anything I had ever eaten before – Mum certainly never made anything similar at home – and it sparked a lifelong fascination with what is essentially a posh

Swiss roll. Occasionally there would one remaining in the chiller at the end of the working day, and if I was extremely lucky it would be offered to me to take home. That was always a very good day.

Tonight, with old friends coming for dinner, I get my chance at a moment of nostalgia. People can be a bit sniffy about tinned fruit these days, but when canned in juice rather than syrup, it can be very good. I used a few hazelnuts, both in the sponge and in the cream, to add a bit more body and crunch, and a splash of peach liqueur from a bottle I found lurking in the cupboard. But apart from that it was pretty much as I remembered it.

Makes 8 generous slices

100g blanched hazelnuts

4 eggs

100g caster sugar, plus extra for coating

75g self-raising flour

400ml double cream

1 tbsp icing sugar

2–3 tbsp peach liqueur (optional)

1 x 400g tin apricot halves in juice, drained & chopped into 1cm pieces

Preheat the oven to 200°C/Gas 6. Grease and line a baking tray of approximately 28 x 40cm and 1cm deep with baking paper.

Add the hazelnuts to a small frying pan and set over a medium heat, shaking the pan from side to side until toasted golden brown all over. Tip into a mortar and roughly crush with the pestle. Spoon about half the nuts into a small dish and set aside. Carry on grinding the remaining nuts until they are finely crushed.

Break the eggs into a large mixing bowl and add the sugar. Using an electric whisk, beat together until they are thick, pale and creamy. You could equally well use a food mixer with the whisk attachment if you have one. Either way it will take a good few minutes – about 8–10. If you lift the whisk and trail a little of the mixture over the surface, and it forms a ribbon that holds its shape for a few seconds, then you know it's ready. This is known as the 'ribbon stage' of cake-making.

Sift over the flour and add the finely ground hazelnuts, and, using a large metal spoon, fold gently in a figure-of-eight motion until just incorporated – take care not to over-mix or you will lose valuable air. Pour into the prepared tin, levelling into the corners, and bake in the oven for 10 minutes.

Cut a large rectangle of baking paper and sprinkle all over with a thin even layer of caster sugar. Once the sponge is ready, remove it from the oven and carefully invert on to the sugared baking paper. Peel off and discard the paper it cooked on. Turn it so that a short side is facing you, and score a line part way through the sponge along this edge, 1cm in. Roll up the sponge tightly around the baking paper and set on a baking tray to cool.

Once the sponge is completely cold, whip the cream with the icing sugar, and liqueur if using, until it is softly billowing rather than stiff. Unroll the sponge, discarding the paper, and spread the cream in an even layer all over. Sprinkle over the reserved hazelnuts and the chopped apricots, pushing them lightly under the surface. Starting from the same end as before, re-roll the sponge around the cream. Place seam-side down on a serving plate and sprinkle over a little more sugar.

25th April

Watercress & brie flamiche

If a quiche and a pizza fell in love, a 'flamiche' would be the probable offspring. It's from northern France, and consists of a thin bread base with an egg-and-cream-rich leek topping. Sometimes the bread is replaced with puff pastry, and occasionally it even acquires a lid, essentially making a leek pie. While I prefer to stick to an open, bread-based tart, I do like to vary the traditional leek topping.

I wilted a bunch of watercress alongside the softened leek to give it a peppery kick, and added a few cubes of ripe brie to melt over as it was cooking. Spinach would be good too, or even some wild garlic.

Enough for 4 for supper or lunch

For the dough:

300ml hand-hot water (use half boiling & half cold)

1 tsp dried yeast

A pinch of caster sugar

450g strong white (bread) flour

½ tsp salt

2 tbsp olive oil, plus extra to grease the bowl

For the topping:

25g butter

1 large leek, washed, trimmed & thinly sliced

170g watercress, well washed & roughly chopped (about 2 bunches)

3 eggs

3 tbsp crème fraîche

A little freshly grated nutmeg

Salt & freshly ground black pepper

125g ripe brie, cubed as best you can depending on how squidgy it is

Measure the water into a jug and sprinkle over the yeast and sugar, stirring well until it has dissolved. Set aside for 10 minutes to allow the yeast a little time to wake up. Weigh the flour into a mixing bowl and stir through the salt. Make a well in the middle and pour in the yeasty water and the olive oil, using a wooden spoon to mix it together into a rough ball. Tip on to the work surface and knead, using the heel of your hands to push, pull and stretch the dough for a generous 5 minutes or so until it is smooth and elastic. Shape into a ball and place in a clean, lightly oiled bowl. Cover and set aside for 30 minutes to prove.

While the dough is rising, cook the topping. Melt the butter over a low heat in a deep frying pan and sweat the leeks gently for around 10–15 minutes until very soft. It is important not to let the leeks burn as they will take on an unpleasant bitter taste. A piece

of baking paper, scrunched up under running water, shaken dry and tucked over the top of the pan, will create a steamy lid that helps them soften without overheating.

Once the leeks are soft, add the watercress and wilt down for just a couple of minutes. Remove from the heat and allow to cool a little. In a small bowl, beat together the eggs and crème fraîche and season well with nutmeg, salt and black pepper. Pour into the leek and watercress mixture and stir well.

Preheat the oven to 200°C/Gas 6.

Tip the ball of dough on to a baking tray lined with baking paper and stretch and shape into a freeform base like a pizza. Using your finger and thumb, press a little indentation 1cm in from the edge all the way round, creating a border that will contain the topping. Pour over the topping and level out with a spoon. Scatter over the cubes of brie and bake for around 20 minutes until puffed up and golden brown on top. Serve warm, cut into generous wedges.

27th April

Crispy bacon, asparagus & egg salad with creamy mustard dressing

Spring marches on apace. The wisteria growing up the front of the house, my botanical pride and joy and a Mother's Day present from my little boy five years ago, is in full bloom now, looking and smelling amazing. The flowers last barely two weeks, yet I spend all year anticipating their glorious explosion of purple and white.

Like the flowering of my wisteria, the start of the English asparagus season is something I long for every year. Asparagus is one of the things I refuse to buy if it's not English. While Spanish strawberries I can deal with occasionally, Peruvian asparagus I cannot. Once the season starts I eat plenty, several times a week, to get my fill. Luckily it is a natural partner to eggs and I can think of numerous ways to make the most of it – tarts and quiches, cheesy asparagus muffins, asparagus 'soldiers' for boiled eggs.

This evening it was *just* warm enough to eat al fresco, and I turned to a simple and quick salad so we could make the most of the last of the day's sun. Using a few odds and sods foraged from a bare fridge, some stale bread and, most satisfyingly, a few handfuls of salad leaves from the first garden harvest, it was ready in a matter of minutes and up the garden we went, glass of wine in hand, thanking the chickens for their contribution to our supper as we passed them.

Serves 2

2 tbsp olive oil

2 cloves garlic, peeled & bruised

2 thick slices of bread, cubed

8 rashers smoked streaky bacon

3 eggs

1 bunch English asparagus, woody ends trimmed

2 generous handfuls salad leaves

For the dressing:

2 generous tbsp good-quality mayonnaise

1–2 tbsp sherry vinegar

1 tbsp wholegrain mustard

Salt & freshly ground black pepper

Warm the oil in a heavy-based frying pan and add the garlic, frying for a few minutes until it is a light golden brown. Remove and discard the garlic, then add the cubes of bread and fry until crisp, tossing about in the oil to ensure they are evenly cooked. Remove to a plate and set aside.

Add the bacon to the pan and fry until crisp, then chop into bite-size pieces and set aside with the croutons.

Boil the eggs to your liking. I like mine just set all the way through, so I submerge them in a pan of cold water, bring it up to a gentle boil and simmer for 5 minutes, starting the timer as soon as the water is simmering. If you like a very soft yolk, cook for 3 minutes, or 4 minutes for a midway point between the two. Peel, cut in half and set aside.

Make the dressing by whisking the mayonnaise, sherry vinegar to taste and wholegrain mustard in a small bowl. Season with a little salt and plenty of black pepper.

Bring a large pan of salted water up to a brisk boil. Cook the asparagus for 3–4 minutes or until just tender but with a little bite. Drain well.

Assemble the salad by arranging the leaves on a plate, topping with the bacon pieces, egg halves, croutons and asparagus. Finally, drizzle over the dressing and eat immediately.

29th April

Stem ginger, raisin & whisky steamed pudding

SWEET COMFORT IN A BOWL

By this time of year, we really shouldn't feel the need to eat wintry comfort puddings. But spring seems to be doing as spring often does, lurching from deliciously warm to positively chilly in a matter of hours. Lulled recently into a false sense of early summer, I only seem to feel the cold even more when it, inevitably, comes. So on this grey drizzly day I am more than happy to keep warm and productive in the kitchen, pottering about and listening to the radio accompanied by the gentle clatter of a pudding steaming on the hob.

The starting point for this pud was the bottle of whisky I found gathering dust in the cupboard, given to my husband two Christmases ago by a very generous work colleague. While he likes the occasional tipple if friends are over, I cannot abide the stuff. I like the *idea* of liking it but, try as I might, I just don't. Whisky feels like a very grown-up drink and maybe I am just not quite ready for it. So into the pan it goes, warmed gently with a generous shake of raisins until the fruit is swollen and succulent. In pudding form it adds just the right note of dusky peaty scent and becomes more than palatable – it was truly delicious, just the ticket to keep the damp and cold at bay.

Makes 6–8 wedges

Butter for greasing

100ml whisky

200g raisins

5 tbsp golden syrup

100g vegetable suet

80g dark brown sugar

50g wholemeal breadcrumbs

50g self-raising flour

2 tsp ground mixed spice

3 eggs

150g stem ginger, finely chopped

Grease a 1-pint pudding basin with butter. You will also need baking paper, string and tin foil.

Pour the whisky into a small saucepan and stir through the raisins. Set over a low heat and warm gently for a few minutes, pushing the fruit under the whisky from time to time. Remove from the heat and set aside for 30 minutes or so until the raisins have absorbed pretty much all of the liquid.

Spoon the golden syrup into the greased pudding basin, and set aside. A measuring spoon dipped into a mug of boiling water will make the job much easier and less messy.

In a large bowl, mix the suet, sugar, breadcrumbs, flour and mixed spice. Beat the eggs in a small bowl. Add the soaked raisins (plus any residual whisky) and the stem ginger and stir through.

Pour into the dry ingredients and mix thoroughly before scraping into the pudding basin. Pat down with the back of a wooden spoon.

Cover with a layer of baking paper and tie securely with string, then cover with a double layer of foil. Carefully lower the pudding into a large pan of hot water, ensuring the water comes no further than halfway up the basin. Cover with a lid and simmer gently for 3 hours, checking every now and then that there is plenty of water in the pan, topping up if necessary.

Carefully take the pudding out of the pan, and remove the foil and baking paper. Run a table knife around the pudding to ease it away from the sides, place a serving plate over the top of the basin, and invert. Serve with custard or cream.

3rd May

Coffee & walnut cake

THE NUMBER ONE CAKE IN THE WORLD

Barely a week goes by without the baking of a cake in our house. Life, I feel, is too short not to eat cake on a regular basis. When I started my great chicken-and-egg adventure, I knew, by the very nature of the subject, that there would be a fair few baking recipes, so I spent some idle time happily musing over what would be my all-time favourite. And here it is. If I could only eat one more piece of cake in my life, it would be generously cut from an old-fashioned coffee and walnut sponge. Coffee anything is a big hit for me (as evidenced by my recipes for mocha éclairs on page 23 and coffee custard on page 245), while the combination of light-as-a-feather sponge, crunchy walnuts and coffee-rich icing is simply sublime. The trick is getting the sponge as airy as you can, for which you

need to cream the butter and sugar together until it is a shade paler than magnolia paint. A food mixer with a paddle attachment is a very valuable tool in the cake lovers' kitchen and will do the job in a few easy minutes. The second best way is in a deep mixing bowl with an electric whisk. I doubt a wooden spoon and copious elbow grease would ever really get the job done, but am happy to be proved wrong if anyone fancies bringing me a slice.

On the subject of icing, my preference is for a generous smear between the sponge layers and another layer on top. To my mind icing the sides is overkill and tips the ratio of icing to sponge in the wrong direction. But if you have a very sweet tooth, increase my quantities for the icing by a third and go the whole hog.

Serves about 8

180g unsalted butter, at room temperature, plus extra for greasing

180g caster sugar

3 eggs

180g self-raising flour

1 tbsp baking powder

2 tbsp very strong black coffee (espresso strength)

1 tsp vanilla extract

75g walnut pieces, roughly chopped

For the icing:

180g unsalted butter, at room temperature

360g icing sugar

2 tbsp very strong black coffee (espresso strength)

35g walnut pieces

Preheat the oven to 180°C/Gas 4. Grease and line the bases and sides of two 20cm loose-based sponge tins.

Preferably in a food mixer, cream together the butter and sugar until very pale and almost fluffy in consistency, scraping down the sides with a spatula from time to time to ensure it all gets mixed.

Add the eggs, one at a time, beating really thoroughly between each addition. Sift over the flour and baking powder, add the coffee and vanilla, and beat one more time on high speed until the batter is light and creamy. Remove the bowl from the mixer, scraping off the beater attachment as you go, scatter over the walnuts and, using a large metal spoon, fold together quickly and gently until it is just combined. Divide between the cake tins and level the surface with the flat of a knife. Bake for about 20–25 minutes until a skewer inserted into the centre comes out clean. Turn out on to a cooling rack and allow to cool completely before icing.

To make the icing, beat the butter in a food mixer (or with an electric whisk) until soft and creamy. Sift over the icing sugar and pour in the coffee and beat again until smooth. Spread half the icing over one sponge, top with the other sponge and spread the rest over, creating a few artful whorls as you go. Scatter the walnuts over the top.

5th May
Crab & egg 'brik'
A GARDEN LUNCH IN THE SPRING SUNSHINE

A 'brik' is an exquisite pastry from Tunisia, and the inspiration for this recipe was two-fold. First, the recipe for a crab brik, with no egg, in the fabulous Moro cookbook, which I have always salivated over but never got round to making. Secondly, the vivid memories I have of eating genuine 'brik à l'oeuf' in Tunisia on holiday as a teenager – crisp, crunchy pastry surrounding soft oozing egg, utter delicious simplicity. The other overriding memory of that holiday is of the plane journey to get there. We flew over the Med, and as we reached land on the other side, Mum jumped up and down shrieking, 'Africa, there's Africa down there,' mortifying me and

my brother into head-burying hormonal silence. Her excitement was no doubt fuelled by the couple of nerve-steadying gins she had consumed during the flight. All these years later, as I make my own brik for the first time, I remember the incident with a wide smile, amazed by the things that are lodged deep down in my memory.

My recipe combines egg with crab for a doubly gorgeous treat. We ate them in the garden bathed in the warm spring sunshine, enveloped contentedly in one of those happy-to-be-alive moments. The yolks of the eggs were super golden, meaning I must have been treating the girls to extra greens. In my short time as a novice hen-keeper I have noticed that extra cabbage equals extra rich and extra yellow, almost orange, yolks.

Makes 4

250g fresh crab meat – ideally half brown meat for flavour & half white meat for texture

4 spring onions, finely sliced

1 red chilli, finely chopped, seeds in or out depending on your preference for heat

Small handful of flat-leaf parsley, chopped

Juice of half a lemon

Salt & freshly ground black pepper

8 sheets of filo pastry

50–75g unsalted butter, melted

4 eggs

Coarse sea salt, to finish

Preheat the oven to 220°C/Gas 7.

In a small bowl, mix together the crab, spring onion, chilli and parsley. Stir through the lemon juice and season to taste with salt and black pepper.

Unroll 2 sheets of the filo and sandwich them together with a little melted butter. Spoon a quarter of the crab mixture into the centre and create a deep indentation in the middle with the back of a teaspoon. Crack an egg into this, then fold one side of the pastry carefully over it. Brush with a little more butter before folding the other side up over the top. You should now have enclosed the filling and be left with a sort of flattened cracker-shape. Brush the surface gently with more butter, then fold up the two 'tails', brushing once again so the surface is well buttered all over.

Place the brik on a baking tray, seam-side down, and repeat with the remaining filo until you have 4 neat parcels. Brush the top surface with a final slick of butter and sprinkle with coarse sea salt. It may feel like you are using a lot of butter, but briks are normally deep-fried, and these baked versions need a generous amount of butter to get the pastry to crisp up in the oven.

Bake in the oven for 12–15 minutes until the pastry is crisp and golden. Serve hot from the oven.

10th May

Huevos revueltos with asparagus & prawns

FANCY EGGS FOR LUNCH

Huevos revueltos is Spanish for 'scrambled eggs', and I find it such a fun name I couldn't resist using it. Every time I read it I am quietly amused and secretly translating it into 'revolting eggs', which they most definitely are not. These are more elaborate than our English version, and can contain all manner of extra ingredients, such as spinach, mushrooms, cured ham, cheese or seafood. They are also eaten as more of a lunch or simple supper dish than a breakfast dish. As a treat for a friend who was coming for lunch, my version today was quite rich and luxurious. Among the eggs nestled pieces of asparagus and big fat prawns cooked in plenty of butter.

I was hoping to eat in the garden – it is nearly the middle of May, after all – but sadly, once again, plans were scuppered by the

unpredictable weather, and dampness in the air kept us inside. It wasn't particularly cold so we were able to eat with the back doors partially open, allowing us to at least enjoy the sound of birdsong on the breeze, which went a little way towards making up for the lack of sunshine.

A little note on butter. I always cook with unsalted butter. It has a higher burn point so is less likely to catch when frying. I add the salt at a later point for seasoning.

Serves 2, with plenty of toast

50g unsalted butter, plus a little extra to finish

1 bunch of asparagus, about 250g, woody ends trimmed, cut into bite-size pieces

3 spring onions, finely sliced

1 large clove garlic, crushed

250g raw peeled prawns

4 eggs, lightly beaten

Salt & freshly ground black pepper

Melt the butter in a deep frying pan, and as soon as it starts to foam add the asparagus, spring onion and garlic. Fry over a medium heat for 2–3 minutes until the asparagus just begins to soften. Then add the prawns and stir-fry for another couple of minutes until they are just pink, taking care not to overcook them or they will toughen up. Finally pour in the eggs and season generously with salt & black pepper. Allow the eggs to cook over a medium-low heat until they begin to set on the bottom, then gently fold and mix together until they are nearly set but still a touch runny. Turn off the heat, stirring through an extra knob of butter, and allow the eggs to finish cooking with the warmth from the pan before serving.

11th May

Fig & oloroso upside-down cake

Not every night, for sure, but certainly some nights I just *need* a pudding – something nice to look forward to once the kids have gone to bed. And tonight is one of those nights. Outside it is sunny but cold and very windy, definitely not al fresco eating weather, so I want something sweet to comfort and warm me as I snuggle up.

Alas, the cupboards and fridge are both fairly bare so I had to wing it a bit. I found a pack of dried figs lurking in the back of a cupboard. A quick snout in the fridge revealed most of a block of butter, plenty to make a decent-sized cake and, most pleasingly, an unopened bottle of my favourite oloroso sherry. So a cake it was, a sort of fig and oloroso syrup upside-down cake. And, of course, a small glass of sherry for the cook. It is Friday after all.

Like many cakes, this one is at its very best when eaten warm, fresh from the oven, perhaps with a dollop of rich Greek yogurt or crème fraîche. Indeed, the day after baking a cake, not being remotely snobbish about these things, I often give my cakes, piece by piece, a 10-second zap in the microwave. Try it – it will revive them no end. I proudly hold my hand up high and admit to using a microwave: not often, but sometimes they are exceedingly useful. And warming cake is a case in point.

Makes 1 cake, cuttable into 6 wedges

250g soft dried figs, cut into 5mm slices

5 tbsp Demerara sugar

50g unsalted butter

6 tbsp dry oloroso sherry

Finely grated zest of 1 lemon

170g unsalted butter, at room temperature

170g caster sugar

2 large eggs

170g plain flour

1 tsp baking powder

1 tsp vanilla extract

1–2 tbsp milk

Preheat the oven to 180°C/Gas 4. Grease and line a 23–25cm solid-based cake tin with baking paper. A springform tin is not ideal as the syrup will leak – if you don't have a solid cake tin, a baking dish would be a good substitute. Scatter the figs in an even layer over the base of the tin and set aside.

Add the Demerara sugar to a heavy-based frying pan with a tablespoon of cold water and warm over a low heat. Give the pan a little shake from time to time to mix the melting granules. As soon as they have melted, add the butter and sherry, taking care as it may spit a little. The sugar may clump up and harden again, but stir gently over a very low heat for a couple of minutes until the butter melts and the syrup comes together as a smooth sauce. Add the lemon zest, stir thoroughly to mix, then pour it over the figs in the cake tin. Set aside while you make the cake batter.

In a food mixer, or with an electric whisk, cream the room-temperature butter and sugar together until light and fluffy. Add the eggs, one at a time, beating each one well in. Sift over the flour and baking powder and pour in the vanilla extract. Fold gently with a large metal spoon, adding just enough milk to make it soft enough to fall off the spoon with ease.

Spoon the batter into the tin over the figs and level with a knife. Bake in the oven for 35–40 minutes or until a skewer inserted in the centre comes out clean. Remove from the oven, and allow to cool for 5 minutes in the tin. Carefully turn out the cake on to a large plate and peel off the baking paper, pressing down any figs that have worked loose. Serve warm.

14th May

Stir-fried vegetable noodles with chilli egg & soy salmon

MONDAY LEFTOVERS

This dish began life as a quick supper to use up some salmon left over from the weekend's barbecue. I'd marinated it in soy, honey and garlic and cooked it over a really hot grill until the outside was sticky, dark and crisp and the inside was just cooked through. The sweet flaky fish was so delicious with the noodles that I have included it here, but please do not feel this is a hard-and-fast recipe. I think this is the kind of meal Mondays were invented for – a handful of roast chicken, beef or pork, or even a few sliced-up cold sausages would all be perfect. Ditto the vegetables. I used a handful of chestnut mushrooms and a bag of pak choi as that's what I found in the fridge. But spring onions, shredded cabbage, sliced peppers or carrots would work well, as would a shake of frozen peas.

If you like things sweet and spicy, and I do, then add another little scatter of chilli flakes to the vegetables when they are stir-frying, and serve with a drizzle of sweet chilli sauce. This recipe is easily doubled up to serve more, and adaptable to suit whatever leftovers you have.

Supper for 2

For the salmon:
1 tbsp dark soy sauce
1 tsp clear honey
1 clove garlic, crushed
2cm fresh ginger, finely grated
1 salmon fillet (about 150g)

For the chilli egg:
2 eggs
1 tsp dark soy sauce
1 tsp toasted sesame oil
A pinch of dried chilli flakes
A pinch of caster sugar
Salt & freshly ground black pepper

For the noodles:
A little vegetable oil, for frying

2–3 shallots, finely sliced

1 clove garlic, finely sliced

2cm fresh ginger, peeled & sliced into fine matchsticks

A handful of chestnut mushrooms, about 4 or 5, sliced

2 heads of pak choi, about 200g, stems thinly sliced and leaves roughly torn

2 blocks dried egg noodles, approx. 140g, cooked according to the packet instructions

To marinate the salmon, mix together the soy, honey, garlic and ginger in a shallow dish. Lay the salmon fillet in the mixture, turning to coat it all over. Cover and set aside for about 30 minutes out of the fridge, or chilled for up to a couple of hours. When you are ready to cook, heat a barbecue or griddle pan until really hot and sear the salmon quickly for a couple of minutes on each side. Reserve any marinating juices to add to the vegetables as they are frying. Remove the fish and allow to cool a little before teasing into large flakes with a fork. Set aside.

In a small bowl, lightly beat together the eggs with the soy, sesame oil, chilli flakes and sugar, and season with salt and black pepper. Set a wok over a high heat and add a splash of vegetable oil. When it is smoking hot, pour in the egg and swirl around the pan so it spreads out in an even layer like a thin omelette. Cook for barely a minute until it has just set, then turn it out on to a small plate, using a fork to break it up into little bite-size pieces. Set aside.

Add another drizzle of oil to the hot wok and stir-fry the shallots for a few minutes until softening and lightly caramelized at the edges. Add the garlic, ginger, mushrooms and sliced pak choi stems, but not the leaves yet, along with a couple of tablespoons of water and any remaining marinade, and stir-fry for a minute or two until the vegetables are soft.

Add the pak choi leaves and wilt for a few seconds, then stir through the cooked noodles, flaked salmon and egg, tossing well until mixed. Serve immediately.

19th May

Greek lemon, egg & asparagus soup

The asparagus season is now in full flow and I am anxious to make the most of it. Today I added some chopped stems to a traditional Greek egg and lemon soup, called *avgolemono*, and they provided a very welcome vegetable crunch to what is quite a rich soup. The egg is added at the end of cooking to thicken and enrich the chicken stock. Use vegetable stock if you prefer it to chicken, but either way home-made is best for flavour.

Serves 4

1 litre chicken or vegetable stock, ideally home-made

125g orzo (rice-shaped pasta)

Juice and finely grated zest of 1 large lemon

1 tsp cornflour

2 eggs

Salt & freshly ground black pepper

1 bunch of asparagus, about 250g, woody ends trimmed, cut into bite-size pieces

A generous handful of flat-leaf parsley, leaves finely chopped

Bring the stock up to the boil in a large saucepan, and add the pasta, stirring well to ensure the grains separate. Simmer steadily until the pasta is almost done, about 5–6 minutes.

Meanwhile, put the lemon juice and zest in a small bowl and sprinkle over the cornflour. Whisk together until well combined, then break in the eggs and season with a little salt and black pepper. Whisk until the eggs are frothy. Set aside.

When the pasta is almost cooked, add the asparagus and simmer for a couple more minutes until just tender. Turn off the heat and stir through the egg and lemon mixture and the parsley. Taste to check the seasoning, and serve immediately.

Indian spiced potato pancakes with coriander & tomato chutney

These savoury pancakes are loosely based on the dosa, a delicious Indian street-food pancake, in which the batter is made with rice and lentil flours and fermented overnight. My recipe is simpler, and uses ordinary wheat flour spiced up with a little turmeric and mustard seeds.

Makes 6 small pancakes, serving 2–3 for dinner or 4–6 as a starter

For the pancakes:
1 egg
200ml milk
80g plain flour
1 tsp mustard seeds
½ tsp ground turmeric
Salt & freshly ground black pepper

For the filling:
2 medium potatoes, cut into 1cm cubes (about 380g total weight)
2 tbsp sunflower or vegetable oil, plus extra for frying the pancakes
1 large red onion, finely chopped
A handful of frozen peas

1 red chilli, finely chopped
1 clove garlic, crushed
2–3 tsp medium-hot curry paste (to taste)
3 heaped tsp mango chutney

For the coriander & tomato chutney:
1 bunch coriander, leaves & fine stalks finely chopped
100g cherry tomatoes, finely chopped
Juice of 1 lime
1 red or green chilli, deseeded & finely chopped
1 clove garlic, crushed
1 tsp caster sugar

Make the pancake batter by putting all the ingredients in a bowl and whisking together until smooth. Set aside to rest while you prepare the filling.

Bring a pan of lightly salted water to the boil. Tip in the potato cubes and boil for 5 minutes, then drain and set aside. Heat the sunflower oil in a deep frying pan and fry the onion over a medium heat until soft and lightly caramelized – about 15 minutes. Add the frozen peas, chilli, garlic and curry paste and season with salt and plenty of black pepper. Stir through the potatoes and cook over a gentle heat for 5 minutes until they are soft and starting to collapse. Taste to check the seasoning, turn off the heat and cover to keep warm.

Make the fresh chutney by combining all the ingredients in a bowl, seasoning to taste. Set aside for the flavours to infuse.

Add a drizzle of sunflower oil to a frying pan and place over a high heat. Pour in a couple of tablespoons of pancake batter and swirl around to coat the base of the pan. Cook for a minute or so until little bubbles form on the surface. Flip over with a palette knife and cook for a minute on the other side. Remove to a plate and keep warm by covering with a clean tea towel. Repeat with the remaining batter.

When you are ready to assemble the pancakes, spread each one with a little mango chutney. Spoon filling on to one quarter and fold one half of the pancake over the other, then over again to form a triangle. Repeat for the rest. Serve immediately, drizzled with the fresh chutney.

26th May

Dawn gardening followed by a bacon & fried egg sarnie

I woke early and couldn't get back to sleep, so I dragged myself up to see in the dawn outside in the garden with a blissfully solitary mug of coffee and a read of yesterday's paper. With no children come, thankfully, no demands. But quiet it was not. The birds, both the chickens and their wild neighbours – the blackbirds, magpies, wood pigeons and a very noisy crow – were exceptionally vocal as they sang, chirped and squabbled in the sunrise. It was such a gorgeous morning that after my caffeine kick-start, I pottered happily in the garden for an hour or so, deadheading flowers, picking out a few weeds and feeding unsuspecting snails to the chickens. The girls particularly loved the gone-to-seed rocket I pulled out and fed them by the handful.

All the early activity made me ravenous, so into the kitchen I went to make breakfast. Crisp smoked bacon (for me, it always has to be smoked) and luscious fried eggs sandwiched between two slices of soft white bloomer. With ketchup, of course. And then the rest of the family appear one by one down the stairs, deliciously warm, bleary-eyed and bed-crumpled, lured by the irresistible smell of cooking bacon. Early morning heaven.

Summer

Lazy days & picnics

Oh, how I long for summer. Endless afternoons in the garden sipping rosé with friends, or perfectly solitary evenings weeding and watering the vegetable bed serenaded by birdsong. Just thinking about the joys of summer makes me happy. I must have been some sort of lizard in a previous life, gaining much energy from the warm rays of the sun.

I am not a particularly efficient kitchen gardener – believe me when I say I have plenty of failures – but it gives me huge pleasure to grow a few things for my family to eat. For a long time I resisted growing fruit and vegetables, reluctant to turn my precious garden into a regimented allotment. Then I had a revelation – I don't need to grow things in straight lines. I sow my seeds in artful drifts, and patchwork my fruit and vegetables among my treasured ornamentals. This is probably not as productive as the 'straight line & neat labels' approach, but it works for me.

One of my big garden successes has been a peach tree fan-trained up a south-facing stone wall. A well-researched and much-longed-for purchase, it has only been in the ground for two complete seasons and it is doing really rather well. The first year I got nine peaches, the second it rewarded me with twenty-three. It is in such a sheltered sunny spot that we can pick the luscious fruit a few weeks earlier than we should. By the end of June or early July I am lucky enough to be sinking my teeth into a ripe home-grown peach.

A bright green scramble of pea plants makes its way up and over the chicken run, the tendrils winding efficiently around the mesh, the leaves and flowers that dare to poke inwards rapidly

June

Proper mayonnaise
Vanilla ice cream with warm
currant sauce
Florentine-style spinach & egg tarts
English 'Niçoise' of smoked trout,
Jersey Royals and asparagus
Gala pie with chorizo
Summer berries & cream shortcake
Tortilla española with smoky
tomato sauce
Empanada gallega
Queen of puddings

July

Almond, apricot & raspberry Danish
Very useful spiced banana cake
Peach & almond cake with lavender
syrup
Crisp cannellini bean & courgette
fritters
American breakfast pancakes
Saffron alioli
Pea, yellow courgette & mint quiche
Gooseberry & elderflower clafoutis
Broad bean, feta & mint omelette

August

Red pepper & goat's cheese tart
Lemon cheesecake with raspberries
Salt & pepper Scotch eggs,
and falafel eggs
Baked rice pudding with greengages
A simple Russian salad
Blackberry & apple parfait with
maple oat crumbs
Curried egg mayonnaise
Chocolate-dipped nougat with candied
orange, honey & almonds

pecked off by the girls, who seem to have astonishing eyesight. By early summer the plants are scattered with abundant pods. Full size but still cardboard-thin, they won't be ready to harvest for a few more tantalizing weeks. The mint that will taste so good with them is looking glorious, full leaved and bushy, but it is almost too healthy, and threatens to overpower the broad beans that are just coming into flower. A vigorous prune should keep it in check, and the chickens will enjoy the offcuts.

The hardest and most constant garden battle comes from the slugs and snails. Our warm and damp climate here in Bristol encourages them to breed, and therefore feed, voraciously. But it is here that the chickens really come into their own. The second best thing about keeping them – after the eggs, of course – is their seemingly insatiable appetite for slugs and snails. After a short summer shower I can often be found bribing the kids, usually with something edible, to go on a slug-hunt around the garden, resulting in a by-the-bucket-load bounty the girls thoroughly enjoy.

Summer cooking should be simple and delicious but low-faff and eminently transportable. These balmy days call for spontaneity in our eating, whether that means dragging a rug and a few cushions up the garden for an impromptu supper, or a proper old-fashioned family 'outing' with a fully laden picnic basket. And let us not forget that, despite our most ardent wishes, we still get plenty of chilly and damp summer days when we should be happy to spend a little more time in the kitchen working wonders with the season's bountiful produce.

Summer is full of bright sunshine recipes to make the most of long days and glorious ingredients.

1st June

Proper mayonnaise

FOR A WHOLE BROWN CRAB

I am perfectly happy with mayonnaise out of a jar, and I dollop it on to all manner of things hot and cold. I'd even go so far as to say that in most circumstances I actually prefer the less-rich, ready-made stuff. Sometimes, however, a bowl of wobbly, glistening, home-made mayo is the only way to go. Tonight I had planned a small celebratory dinner for the two of us, a 'love meal' if you like, a chance to eat, drink, share and talk, for no other reason than it had been a glorious day and sometimes it feels good to make an effort. As multi-tasking, stretched-to-the-point-of-snapping grown-ups, it's all too easy to collapse in front of the box night after night after night.

On the menu was a large brown crab, to be cracked and picked, its juicy flesh to be squeezed with lemon and dunked in mayo, accompanied by no more than good bread and plenty of wine.

Mayonnaise is easy-peasy to knock up. The main skills required are patience and a steady hand. The key is adding the oil almost painfully slowly, drop by frustrating drop, and allowing it time to emulsify with the egg before adding more. For this reason I make it in my food mixer while having another mundane task to occupy myself, usually loading or unloading the dishwasher. That way you leave the motor running, add a drop of oil, and step away for a good few seconds, thus resisting the temptation to over-pour during the critical early stages.

Makes a dessert-bowlful, plenty for 4–6

2 egg yolks

1 heaped tsp Dijon mustard

200ml groundnut oil

50ml extra virgin olive oil

1–2 tbsp white wine vinegar, to taste

Salt & freshly ground black pepper

Put the egg yolks and Dijon mustard into the bowl of a food mixer, or a deep mixing bowl if you are using an electric or balloon whisk. Whisk together until completely combined. Measure the oils into a jug and, with the whisk running, add literally a drop to the egg yolks. Put the jug down and keep on whisking for a few seconds, before adding another drop. Repeat a few more times until you see the egg yolk thickening a little and turning paler, then you can increase the flow of oil to two or three drops each time. Always make sure you have completely whisked the oil into the emulsion before adding any more. Once about half the oil is in, the mixture should look thick and dense. At this point add a tablespoon of vinegar and whisk to thin it out a little, then go back to adding the oil a few drops at a time. Once all the oil is in, season to taste with salt and black pepper, and a little more vinegar to sharpen as necessary. Spoon into a bowl and chill until needed.

4th June

Vanilla ice cream with warm currant sauce

Eighteen months ago I planted four currant bushes, two each of red and black, with a view to making the king of all puds – summer pudding. How laughably naive I was. The birds have other ideas, which I suppose is why such things as fruit cages exist. The first year's harvest was a mere handful of berries from each bush, and this year's is not much better, just a small bowlful – not even enough for a mouse-sized summer pudding. Still, it gave me an idea for a simple and sublime dessert – warm currant sauce, fragrant and deep claret coloured, poured over rich sweet vanilla ice cream. What better way to showcase the glorious yellow of the egg yolks than with a classic custard-based ice cream. While I was stirring slowly – for there is a lot of stirring involved in custard making – I remembered fondly the vivid yellow Bird's custard powder we always had when I was little, and felt more than a little smug that my eggs made a custard this yellow without the use of any additives. You will need an ice-cream maker for this – I use one with a removable bowl that I leave in the freezer so it's ready whenever I get the urge to make ice cream. Which is not terribly often, I have to say, but it's nice to be ready just in case . . .

Makes about 500ml ice cream and enough sauce for 2

For the vanilla ice cream:
300ml double cream
200ml milk
1 vanilla pod, split lengthways
125g caster sugar
5 egg yolks

For the currant sauce:
140g mixed currants
2 tbsp granulated sugar
2 tbsp water

In a small pan, heat the cream and milk with the vanilla pod until just below boiling point. Turn off the heat and allow to infuse for 30 minutes. Scrape out the seeds of the vanilla pod into the creamy milk and discard the pod.

Weigh the sugar into a large, preferably metal, bowl and whisk in the egg yolks. Pour the vanilla-scented milk over the eggs and whisk together. Wash the saucepan out then pour the uncooked custard back into it. Wash and dry the metal bowl and stand it in a sink of cold water with a clean whisk. This is your insurance policy should the custard threaten to split due to over-heating. As the bowl is metal it will allow the heat to be quickly dissipated.

Set the pan over a really low heat and stir the custard constantly with a wooden spoon. In time it will thicken – be patient, it can take 10 minutes or more. Do not take your eyes off it, and do not be tempted to speed up the process by increasing the heat. Should it look like it is about to curdle, pour immediately into the metal bowl in the sink and whisk vigorously to bring it all back together, then carry on with a little more vigilance.

When the custard has thickened, transfer to a bowl, seal with a layer of clingfilm to prevent skin forming, cool, then chill in the fridge. When completely cold, transfer to your ice-cream maker and churn according to the instructions. Scrape into a freezable container and store until needed.

To make the currant sauce, simply simmer everything together in a small saucepan until the currants are soft but not mushy. Taste and add a little more sugar if the sauce is too tart, but remember it's to be poured over really sweet ice cream so a certain level of sharpness is a good thing. Spoon the warm sauce over a scoop or two of cold ice cream and eat immediately.

7th June

Florentine-style spinach and egg tarts

Supper was another of what has become affectionately known as the 'freezer special' in our house – a last-minute rummage around the over-frosted drawers to see what can be salvaged and combined to make something quick to eat. I feel I have become expert at the 'something out of nothing' school of cooking. Most of my working life is spent either cooking or writing about cooking and eating. Often I forget that we, as a family, need to eat too. Today's forage yielded half a bag of frozen spinach bricks and half a block of puff pastry, providing the inspiration I needed to whip up these tarts – a

sort of Italian Fiorentina pizza crossed with a Greek spanakopita. Pan-European savouriness at its best. Feel free to use fresh spinach if you are more organized than me. But a few choice frozen vegetables – peas, broad beans and spinach – are a useful thing to have tucked away. You just never know when you might need them.

Makes 2 generous individual tarts

5 'bricks' frozen spinach (yielding approx. 150g when defrosted & squeezed of excess water) or 500g fresh spinach

2 tbsp olive oil

1 onion, finely chopped

2 cloves garlic, crushed

100g feta cheese, crumbled

Freshly grated nutmeg

Sea salt & freshly ground black pepper

250g (½ block) puff pastry

2 large eggs

Preheat the oven to 220°c/Gas 7.

Defrost the spinach and squeeze out as much of the water as you can. I use the microwave for both speed and convenience. Set aside. If you are using fresh spinach, wilt it in a covered pan with the minimum of water, then drain and squeeze.

Heat the olive oil and gently sweat the onion for 10 minutes or so until soft and translucent. Add the garlic and fry for a further minute before stirring in the squeezed spinach. Remove from the heat and fold through the crumbled feta. Season to taste with nutmeg, salt and pepper.

Cut the pastry into 2, then roll each piece into a 2–3mm-thick shape of your liking – neat square or wiggly freeform oval, it matters not – and lightly score a 1cm margin all around the edge. Transfer to a baking tray, brush the edges with a little water and sprinkle over a few flakes of sea salt. Divide the spinach between the 2 tarts, taking care not to let it spill over into the margin. Using a spoon, make a well in the centre of each, crack in the egg and finish with a final grind of black pepper.

Bake in the oven for 15–20 minutes until the pastry is crisp and the egg cooked to your liking.

10th June

English 'Niçoise' of smoked trout, Jersey Royals and asparagus

A SIMPLE SALAD TO END A SUNNY DAY

The perfect English summer's day is a rare and wonderful thing indeed, cloudless sunny skies and warm breezes stretching into a seemingly endless balmy evening. Today is such a treat of a day. And as a bonus the kids are on holiday too, so into the car we go, snacks and drinks stuffed in a rucksack, for a family outing to a National Trust house where there are wonderful kitchen gardens for the grown-ups, rather expensive ice creams and plenty of charging around space for the kids. Everyone's a winner. And as a massive bonus, on the way home we stumbled unexpectedly on a smokery producing the most delicate, pale-fleshed smoked trout I have ever seen. After much tasting, I bought a generous fillet for supper, to be eaten, of course, in the garden – eating outside is essential when the weather is this lovely. The perfect end to a perfect day.

With such a lovely piece of fish it seemed only sensible to showcase it with just a few other prime seasonal goodies, not so much a recipe as an idea. So I made a simple salad by flaking the trout over warm Jersey Royal potatoes and asparagus, served on a bed of mixed leaves and herbs from the garden and topped with halves of soft-boiled egg. I came to think of it as an English version of that French classic, the Niçoise salad. I dressed the leaves simply with some good olive oil and lemon juice, but I wanted a punchy, creamy dressing for the fish so I mixed a generous spoon of grated horseradish into some crème fraîche with a handful of chives.

15th June
Gala pie with chorizo

Gala pie – essentially a pork pie with boiled eggs nestled in the centre – is a tasty picnic dish. It travels well with its sturdy pastry shell. As a child, I remember watching slices of gala pie being cut at the supermarket deli counter. The seemingly endless tube of egg was fascinating, and to this day I have no idea how they extrude eggs into long sausage shapes. I think I prefer not to know. Thankfully, my Spanish-inspired version contains genuine whole boiled eggs, which does mean the slicing is a bit of a roulette. Not everyone gets the egg they may desire. My advice is to cut as thin as you can so people might have room for not one but two slices.

The meaty filling tastes best if it is left to marinate overnight in the fridge for the flavours to intensify and mingle. If you are short of time, at least leave it for a couple of hours. Then, once the pie has been baked, it needs to rest again overnight in the fridge – much patience is required for this dish. But as a once-in-a-while treat it is well worth it. I think pork pies of any kind demand some sort of piquant sauce to eat alongside – piccalilli or rich onion chutney would be ideal.

Serves 5–6

For the pie filling:

375g rindless meaty pork belly, cut into 1cm cubes

275g smoked gammon, cut into 1cm cubes

200g chorizo, cut into 1cm cubes

3 tbsp sherry vinegar

5 tbsp cold water

2 bay leaves, finely chopped (fresh or dried)

1 tsp ground mace

1 tsp ground white pepper

1 tsp cumin seeds

1 tsp dried thyme

1 tsp smoked paprika

3 eggs, hard-boiled & peeled

Sea salt & freshly ground black pepper

For the hot water crust pastry:
400g plain flour, plus extra for dusting

1 tsp fine salt

1 egg

170ml water

80g lard

80g butter

For the jelly:
1 ham stock cube

2 sheets of leaf gelatine (4g) or same weight of powdered

200ml boiling water

In a large mixing bowl, mix the pork belly, gammon and chorizo, then transfer approximately half to a food processor. Add the sherry vinegar and cold water and process until a coarse paste is formed. Add the bay leaves, mace, white pepper, cumin, dried thyme and paprika, and season generously with salt and black pepper. Scrape back into the mixing bowl, and, with clean hands, mix and squidge the two lots of meat together so they are well combined. Cover with clingfilm and rest in the fridge overnight, or for a minimum of 2 hours.

Once the meat has marinated, begin the pastry. Add the flour and salt to a mixing bowl, make a deep well in the centre and crack in the egg, using the empty shell to cover the surface with flour so it is hidden. Measure the water into a small saucepan and add the lard and butter. Set over a medium heat and bring up to the boil, stirring often to ensure the fat melts quickly. As soon as the water comes up to the boil, pour into the flour, mixing with a metal spoon as you do so. Using your hands, briefly knead the dough into a smooth ball, wrap tightly in clingfilm and chill in the fridge until cool and firm but not too firm to roll – around 30–45 minutes.

Line a large (2lb) loaf tin with a double thickness of baking paper, leaving two tails at each end to help lift the cooked pie out. Cut a third off the ball of dough and set aside. On a lightly floured worktop, roll the remaining two-thirds of dough into a rough rectangle about 5–7mm thick. Carefully lift it and line the tin, pressing firmly into the corners and ensuring any cracks or tears are pressed back together. Using a small sharp knife, trim the pastry, leaving a 1cm overhang around the rim.

Put about half the marinated meat into the tin, pressing firmly down to ensure no gaps. Lay the peeled hard-boiled eggs along the centre, then top with the remaining meat, pressing around and over the eggs so they are covered and hidden.

Roll out the reserved pastry to form a lid 1cm bigger than the surface of the tin, and lay over the meat. Bring up the overhanging pastry and press and crimp the edges together to seal. Make 3 pen-sized holes in the top, into which the jellied stock is poured once the pie has cooked. To help keep them open during cooking, roll little tubes of foil – using something like a pen or pencil to roll them around – and poke into the holes.

Bake in the oven at 160°C/Gas 3 for about 1½ hours until the meat has cooked and the pastry is a deep golden brown. If you have a meat thermometer, the internal temperature should be 75°C. If you don't, take the pie out of the oven, insert a metal skewer into its centre and leave for 10 seconds, then remove and immediately touch the tip to your lip. If it feels hot, it's done; if not, return to the oven for 10 minutes before testing again.

Make jellied stock by combining all the ingredients in a jug, stirring until the gelatine has dissolved. Set aside to cool. Allow the cooked pie to cool for 1 hour before pouring in the jellied stock. Use a funnel to guide it into the holes, working slowly so it soaks down rather than explodes over. Allow to cool completely, in the tin, before refrigerating overnight.

Release the pie from the tin by running a knife around the edges and using the baking paper tails to lift it out.

18th June

Summer berries & cream shortcake

TO CHEER UP A DRIZZLY DAY

On a damp and dreary so-called summer's morning, sports day had just been cancelled for the second time due to the famous Bristol drizzle. I made this cake to cheer up a disappointed six-year-old for whom performing at sports day in front of his dad was to be the highlight of the term. This gorgeous, indulgent, summery cake is based on the American-style shortcake, a sort of hybrid between a scone and a biscuit, rather than the crisper Scottish shortbread. I love them both, but to my mind this one is marginally easier to eat when it sandwiches a pile of berries and softly whipped cream. You could easily adapt this recipe to make individual shortcakes, but I wonder if that would be missing the point – the glory of this cake is the 'Wow' you get when you present the towering confection to your loved ones. I used a mixed tumble of strawberries and raspberries on my shortcake. Blueberries, loganberries or blackberries would be good too.

Serves 6

275g plain flour, plus extra for dusting

25g polenta

75g caster sugar

1 tbsp baking powder

A pinch of salt

125g unsalted butter, cold & cut into 1cm cubes

150ml full-fat crème fraîche

1 large egg

For the filling:

200g raspberries

200g strawberries

2 tbsp caster sugar

250ml double cream

1 tbsp icing sugar, plus a little extra to dust

1 tsp vanilla extract

Preheat the oven to 180°C/Gas 4. Line 2 baking trays with paper.

In a food processor, pulse the dry ingredients until they are thoroughly mixed. Add the cubes of cold butter and whizz to a breadcrumb texture. Take care not to over-process, or the result will be a tough not tender shortcake. You could do this by hand – rubbing gently between finger and thumb as if making pastry the old-fashioned way. But as it's important not to get the butter too warm, I find it more reliable to quickly use a food processor.

In a jug, measure the crème fraîche, beat in the egg, then pour into the processor and pulse until just combined to a dough. Don't overdo the mixing: less is definitely more in this case. Turn the dough on to a floured worktop, cut in half and roll each half lightly into a ball. Using your palm, press and turn gently until you have a disc about 1cm thick and the size of a Victoria sponge tin – about 23–25cm.

Carefully lift and slide each circle on to the lined trays and bake for around 10–12 minutes until risen and golden brown. While still warm, cut one disc into 8 wedges. Set aside to cool on a wire rack while you prepare the filling.

Mix the raspberries, strawberries and caster sugar in a large bowl and set aside for a few minutes. In another large bowl whip the cream with the icing sugar and vanilla extract – you are looking for soft, delicately whipped peaks, not stiff solid cream.

Once the shortcakes are completely cold, place the whole disc on a serving plate. Pile the cream on top and spread out with the flat of a knife. Top with the fruit and arrange the wedges of shortcake around in a fan, sprinkling all over with a little extra icing sugar. I found it best to use only 7 of my 8 wedges, that number seeming to fit more neatly over the filling – leaving the extra wedge as a little chef's perk with a cup of coffee.

This cake is best eaten the day you make it – it will lose a certain something if it sees the inside of a fridge. But if you do need to chill it, make sure to bring it to room temperature before serving. Or failing that, a few seconds per slice in the microwave will have a miraculous effect.

The First 'Egg Supper'

Today I am running my first ever supper club. Through word-of-mouth and social media advertising, I am expecting eighteen guests, mostly strangers, at my home for an evening of food, drink and merriment. The last few days have been spent cleaning and clearing the detritus of family life out of my kitchen and dining room. I am finding that opening up my home, the place where I truly relax and kick back, is more nerve-wracking than the cooking. The food is the easy bit. On the menu is a feast of Spanish and North African flavours: home-made curd cheese with garlic and sumac, beetroot and walnut pâté with coriander, parsley and mint, flatbreads with nigella and caraway, spiced merguez sausages and Moorish pork skewers, empanadas and classic Spanish tortilla, along with all sorts of salads, and finally rosewater meringues and vanilla ice cream for pudding. Here are two of my very favourite, egg-based, recipes from the evening.

Tortilla española with smoky tomato sauce

Making a Spanish omelette can be a touch tricky, prone as they are to sticking stubbornly to the bottom of the pan. I find there is a delicate balance between cooking the potatoes just long enough so they are melting, but not so long that they go mushy and make the sticking problem all the worse. But I love tortilla, and through much trial and error over the years I have discovered a few tricks to increase my chances of success.

Serves 2–3 generously, or 8 as part of a tapas spread

For the tortilla:
600g potatoes, peeled & cut into 5mm slices

6 tbsp olive oil

1 large onion, chopped

6 large eggs, beaten

Salt & freshly ground black pepper

For the smoky tomato sauce:
3 cloves garlic, crushed

2 tbsp olive oil

600g ripe tomatoes

1 tbsp sherry vinegar

1 tsp smoked paprika (*pimentón*), either the hot or sweet variety

1 tsp sugar, or to taste

Rinse the potato slices under running water to wash away some of the starch, then add them to a large pan and cover generously with cold water. Season with a shake of salt and bring up to the boil. Once boiling, cook for a mere minute, then drain and set aside.

Heat 2 tablespoons of the olive oil in a medium-sized, preferably non-stick, frying pan. Add the onion and sweat it over a low heat for a generous 10–15 minutes until sweet and soft. Add the drained potatoes and continue to cook until the potatoes are soft but still holding their shape. Transfer the potatoes and onions to a bowl and wash and dry the frying pan thoroughly – an important step to minimize sticking.

Return the pan to the hob and heat another 2 tablespoons of olive oil until it is really hot. Season the beaten egg generously with black pepper and a little salt, pour over the potato mixture and stir thoroughly. Pour into the frying pan, reduce the heat to medium and cook for around 5 minutes to set the base. Use a wooden or silicone spatula to loosen the sides as it cooks, and give the pan a little shake from time to time to try to loosen the bottom. It may need a bit of encouraging with the spatula.

Once you feel confident the bottom has set, it's time for the interesting bit. Take a plate that is substantially bigger than the frying pan, lay it over the pan and carefully but quickly invert the whole lot, allowing the tortilla to fall on to the plate. Wash and dry the pan once again, return to the hob and heat the remaining 2 tablespoons of oil. Slide the tortilla back in, cooked side up, and cook for a few more minutes until it feels just set. Invert on to a clean plate and set aside, covered in foil to keep warm (although I find tortillas are best eaten at something nearing room temperature), while you make the sauce.

To make the tomato sauce, fry the garlic in the olive oil for a minute or two until it is just beginning to soften. Take care not to overcook it as burnt garlic is bitter. Add the tomatoes, sherry vinegar and paprika and bring up to a steady simmer. Cook for a good 30–40 minutes until the sauce is thick and jammy. Add a little sugar, tasting as you go, to get a good balance between rich, sweet tomatoes and sharp vinegar.

Serve the warm tortilla in thick wedges with a little of the sauce on the side.

Empanada gallega

A TUNA, EGG & SWEET PEPPER PIE

Empanada gallega is a large flat pie filled with sweetly cooked onions, peppers, tuna and hard-boiled eggs, hailing from Galicia in north-west Spain. With its rich firm crust, a sort of a cross between pastry and bread, it's the perfect thing to take on a picnic – I guess it's the Spanish version of a Cornish pasty. But today, for my supper club, I am not making a large pie as I would normally do but smaller individual pies, or empanadillas, to add to my tapas-inspired egg-feast.

The dough in this recipe is loosely based on one from Jenny Chandler's lovely book *The Food of Northern Spain* – in fact, it was Jenny who first taught me how to cook them when I helped her with a cookery demonstration.

Makes 1 large pie for 6–8 or about 12 individual pasties

For the dough:

1 tsp dried yeast

4 tbsp hand-hot water (use half boiling & half cold), plus extra for binding the dough

350g strong white flour

125g fine polenta

A pinch of salt

100ml white wine

25ml olive oil, plus extra for greasing the bowl

50g lard or vegetable fat, cut into small dice

1 egg, beaten

For the filling:

4 tbsp olive oil

3 large onions, sliced

3 large peppers, I used 1 each of red, green & yellow, thinly sliced

3 cloves garlic, crushed

1 tsp smoked paprika

1 tbsp sherry vinegar

A bunch of flat-leaf parsley, chopped

Salt & freshly ground black pepper

2 x 200g tins tuna fish, drained

3 hard-boiled eggs, sliced

To glaze the pastry:

1 egg, beaten

Flakes of sea salt

Activate the yeast by mixing it with the warm water in a small bowl and leaving for 10 minutes – it should start gently bubbling.

Either by hand, or in a food mixer with a dough attachment, mix together the flour and polenta with the salt. Pour in the wine and olive oil, add the lard or fat, egg and activated yeast. Add enough extra warm water to bring it all together into a soft pliable dough. Knead for a couple of minutes, but don't overdo it – it just needs to be well mixed and look smooth. If you over-knead it can become a little tough on baking. Transfer into a clean bowl that you have brushed with a little oil and cover with clingfilm. Leave to rise until it has doubled in size – an hour or so in a warm room.

While the dough is rising, make the filling. Heat the olive oil gently in a large deep frying pan. Sweat the onions and peppers together for 15 minutes until starting to soften, then add the garlic, paprika and sherry vinegar. Continue to cook until you have a softly melting mass – the longer and slower you do this, the sweeter the result, so take your time: an hour over a very low heat would not be excessive. Stir through the parsley and season to taste. Gently fold through the tuna, trying not to break it up too much. Turn off the heat and set aside.

Preheat the oven to 200°C/Gas 6.

If you are making a large pie, cut the dough in half and roll each half into a large square-ish shape of about 5mm thick. Lay one piece on a baking tray, pile the filling on top and spread out, leaving a generous 2cm margin around the edge. Top with the slices of egg before laying over the second sheet of dough. Crimp and fold the edges together to seal in the filling, then brush with the beaten egg. Scatter over a few flakes of sea salt. To make small empanadillas, roll out the dough and, using a saucer, cut out circles, rerolling the scraps and cutting again until the dough is used up. You should get 12–13 circles, depending on the size of the saucer. Spoon the filling on one half of a circle, top with a slice of egg, fold the dough over and crimp to seal. Brush with egg, sprinkle with sea salt and continue with the remainder.

Bake for 30 minutes for the large empanada, or about 20 minutes for the empanadillas, until the crust is golden and crisp. Best served at room temperature, if you can wait that long.

30th June

Queen of puddings

This is a truly old-fashioned and thoroughly British pudding, the sort of thing American tourists go crazy for. I imagine the name helps. But it is an absolute classic. Simple humble ingredients – milk, eggs, sugar, breadcrumbs and jam – are given the royal treatment, and the pudding comes out of the oven far more than the sum of its frugal parts. And it's just the sort of something-from-nothing dish that goes down a treat in this house.

Serves 4–6, depending on the size of your ramekins

300ml milk

1 tsp vanilla extract

60g caster sugar

3 egg yolks

100g fresh breadcrumbs

Finely grated zest of 1 large lemon

4 tbsp raspberry jam

For the meringue topping:

3 egg whites

100g caster sugar

Preheat the oven to 160°C/Gas 3.

Warm the milk with the vanilla extract until just below boiling point. While the milk is warming, whisk together the caster sugar and egg yolks in a large mixing bowl. Pour over the milk, stirring continuously as you do so. Stir through the breadcrumbs and lemon zest, then spoon the mixture into ramekins, filling about three-quarters of the way to the top. Put the ramekins on a baking tray for ease of transfer, and slide into the oven. Cook for 10 minutes – they should be just about set with a slight custardy wobble. Remove from the oven and increase the temperature to 180°C/Gas 4.

Spoon the jam into a small bowl and stir briskly to thin it a little, then spoon over each of the puddings, smoothing into an even layer.

To make the meringue topping, whisk the egg whites in a squeaky-clean bowl until they are stiff. Add about a third of the sugar and whisk again until smooth and glossy, followed by the remaining sugar in thirds, whisking well between each addition. Spoon or pipe the meringue in generous swirls on top of the jam. Bake in the oven for about 10 minutes until the top is crisp and lightly browned. Serve immediately.

2nd July

Almond, apricot & raspberry Danish

If you have never eaten a home-made Danish pastry, I urge you to give this a go. Buttery, rich, flaky pastry, topped with sweet almond paste and sharp fresh fruit – a truly wonderful breakfast treat to make for a special day. The best thing is that you get all the rolling and shaping done the day before you want to eat them, and then you leave them to prove overnight in the fridge. All you have to do in the morning is heat up the oven and shove them in to cook while you make the coffee. And voilà, a decadent breakfast in minutes.

Fresh apricots are a true summer delight and this year I planted a small tree, a Petit Muscat variety, in a warm sheltered corner of the garden, at right angles to the peach tree that has been such a roaring success. Like the peach, I plan to fan-train it to encourage maximum fruit in the minimum of space, and with a bit of luck this time next year I may be harvesting my own sweet apricots.

Makes 6 pastries

For the dough:

110ml milk

1 tsp dried yeast

2 tsp caster sugar

1 egg, plus 1 yolk (save the extra white to glaze)

1 tsp almond extract

250g plain flour, plus extra for dusting

A pinch of salt

150g butter, cut into 1cm cubes, softened to room temperature

For the filling:

50g caster sugar, plus extra to finish

50g ground almonds

50g butter

½ tsp almond extract

3 fresh apricots, sliced in half, stone removed

A good handful of raspberries

1 egg white, to glaze

Warm the milk to blood temperature – 30 seconds in the microwave or a minute or so in a small saucepan on the hob should do it. Test the temperature by dipping in the tip of a clean little finger: it should feel pleasantly warm and definitely not hot. Sprinkle over the dried yeast and caster sugar, stirring well until dissolved. Set aside for 10–15 minutes until a slight head forms on the surface.

In a small bowl whisk together the egg yolk, whole egg and almond extract. Add the flour to a large mixing bowl and sprinkle over a little salt. Make a well in the centre of the flour and pour in the yeasty milk and the beaten egg. Use a metal spoon to bring the dough together into a rough ball, then tip on to the work surface and knead gently with the heel of your hands for a couple of minutes until it comes together in a smooth ball. Lightly dust the work surface with flour and roll out into a rectangle of about 5mm thick.

Dot the top two-thirds of the dough's surface with the butter cubes, leaving a generous 1cm margin all around the edge butter-free. Fold the unbuttered third up towards the middle, then bring the top third down over that, pressing the edges firmly together to seal the butter in. Give the dough a quarter turn so that the top edge is now facing sideways. Dust with a little more flour and roll into a rectangle, then fold in three as before. Repeat the rolling and folding once more, then chill in the fridge for 30 minutes. After chilling, repeat the rolling and folding cycle three more times, before chilling again for another 30 minutes.

While the dough is having its final rest in the fridge, make the almond paste by creaming together the sugar, ground almonds, butter and almond extract with a fork in a small bowl.

Once the dough has rested, roll out into a large rectangle of about 40 x 30cm, dusting the work surface with a little extra flour to stop it sticking. Cut into 6 pretty much equal pieces and scrape a spoonful of the almond paste into the middle of each, flattening with a knife. Lay an apricot half in the centre, cut side down, and bring up the corners of the dough to meet the edge of the apricot, crimping and pressing down firmly to stick it together. Scatter 3 or 4 raspberries around the apricot. Brush the surface of the pastry with the egg white and sprinkle on a little caster sugar. Spread the pastries out over 2 baking trays and leave to prove overnight in the fridge. If you want to cook them the same day, an hour's proving at room temperature is enough.

Preheat the oven to 200°C/Gas 6. Bake the pastries for 12–15 minutes until deep golden brown. Eat warm from the oven.

6th July
Very useful spiced banana cake

We often have sad-looking bananas in the fruit bowl – Izaac cannot stand them, even the smell turns him green around the gills, and while Eve loves them, she, being three, only eats half at a time. And I love them too but find they are only *perfect* during a very narrow window. I don't enjoy them even a little under-ripe, or a little over-ripe: in the words of Goldilocks, they have to be just right. So it's good to have a great cake recipe to use them up. It's worth noting that bananas freeze really well peeled but left whole, so if you don't have the time or inclination to make a cake, bag them up and freeze for another day. They will look incredibly unpromising on defrosting, a brown slimy mess, but I promise they will make you a gorgeous cake.

Over-ripe bananas create a wonderful, soft squidgy cake that keeps well for several days. Their sweet moisture means you don't need to add too much butter, egg or sugar. So in cake terms this could be considered a healthy option, but it is by no means a dull one. All in all, a simple and most useful recipe to have up your sleeve.

Makes 1 cake, cuttable into 9 or so squares

500g over-ripe bananas (about 3)

125g butter, at room temperature

125g soft dark brown sugar, plus extra for sprinkling over the top

2 eggs

180g plain flour

100g plain wholemeal flour

60g walnuts

60g raisins

3 tsp mixed spice

1 tbsp baking powder

1 tsp bicarbonate of soda

1–2 tbsp milk

Preheat the oven to 170°C/Gas 3. Grease a square cake tin, about 25cm. If the tin is inclined to stick, line it as well. Mash the banana in a bowl then set aside. In a food mixer, or by hand, beat together the butter and sugar. Add the eggs, both flours, walnuts and raisins, mixed spice, baking powder and bicarbonate of soda. Beat until smooth. Add the banana and beat again, then add enough milk to get a soft, dropping consistency.

Pour into the prepared cake tin and sprinkle with a little extra soft brown sugar for a sweet crunchy crust. Bake for 35–40 minutes or until a skewer inserted in the centre comes out clean. Turn out and cool a little on a wire rack. Great served still warm.

11th July

Peach & almond cake with lavender syrup

The initial motivation for baking this cake was an aesthetic one. I was desperate to encapsulate the gorgeousness of my lavender flowers in something edible. And because the lavender grows in a

loose hedge under the peach tree, it made sense to me to pair them in a rich and fragrant cake. As it turned out, the flowers, while infusing the syrup with a lovely, almost ginger-like note, added little in the looks department, having darkened deeply on cooking. My solution was to strain the lavender-flavoured syrup and sprinkle over a few fresh vibrant flowers at the end. You, and the bees that like them so much, may feel this is an unnecessary step, but for me the enjoyment of eating starts in the first instance with the way my food looks. This is what I think of as a 'pudding cake', a generous dollop of crème fraîche elevating it firmly into grown-up after-dinner territory.

Serves 6–8

For the lavender syrup:

180g caster sugar

20g fresh lavender flowers, about 4 tbsp (pick tight, deeply coloured buds)

100ml cold water

For the cake:

225g unsalted butter, at room temperature

225g caster sugar

3 eggs

150g ground almonds

100g plain flour

1 tsp baking powder

500g peach flesh – about 3–4 large peaches – cut into bite-size pieces

A few extra lavender flowers to garnish (optional)

Preheat the oven to 180°C/Gas 4. Line and grease a 23–25cm springform tin.

Make the syrup by bringing all the ingredients to the boil in a small heavy-based saucepan. Simmer for 5 minutes, then turn off the heat and allow to infuse while you get on with the cake.

Beat the butter and sugar together until light and fluffy. The easiest way to do this is in a food mixer or with an electric beater, but a wooden spoon and plenty of elbow grease will do the job for the more energetic.

Add the eggs, one at a time, mixing well between each addition. Tip in the almonds, flour and baking powder and fold together until well combined. Finally fold the peach flesh gently through the cake batter. Pour into the prepared cake tin and bake for about 45–50 minutes, or until a skewer inserted into the centre comes out clean.

Remove the cake from the oven and pour over the strained syrup, then allow the cake to cool in the tin a little before you try to remove it. Decorate with a few fresh lavender flowers scattered over the top, which your guests can eat, or simply admire before discreetly picking off . . .

13th July

Crisp cannellini bean & courgette fritters

A GARDEN SUPPER

These are not the quickest of things to make, but they are mighty fine, and a splendid way of using up a glut of courgettes. Sometimes I want an instant supper, and sometimes I am happy to potter in the kitchen, doors thrown open to the evening birdsong, glass of wine in hand, taking my time over the cooking. Often the process of cooking adds to the pleasure of eating, and I think these savoury and crisp little fritters are a case in point. We ate them in the garden at dusk, with the rest of the wine, accompanied by a perfectly simple tomato salad – thick room-temperature wedges of tomato drizzled with a little of my best olive oil and a generous grinding of salt and pepper. On our way past the run we let the chickens out for a peck-about before they took themselves back to their coop.

Makes 8 smallish fritters, enough for 2 hungry people, with a few leftovers for lunch the next day

250g gold or green courgettes (approx. 2 small–medium)

1 tsp fine salt

2 tbsp olive oil

1 medium onion, finely diced

A generous sprig of rosemary, chopped

2 cloves garlic, crushed

1 x 400g tin cannellini beans, drained & rinsed

100g mozzarella, cut into 1cm cubes

3 tbsp freshly grated Parmesan

1 tbsp balsamic vinegar

Small bunch of basil, roughly chopped

Freshly ground black pepper

2 eggs

1 tbsp plain flour

4 tbsp breadcrumbs

Vegetable or olive oil for shallow-frying

Grate the courgettes into a sieve and mix with a teaspoon of fine salt. Hang over a bowl and place a weight on top – I found another bowl and a cast-iron pestle & mortar did the job well; a tin or two of baked beans is another good option. Set aside for 30 minutes to drain, then squeeze out as much juice as possible.

Heat the oil in a frying pan and gently sweat the onion with the rosemary for 10 minutes or so until soft and slightly caramelized. Add the garlic and fry for another minute. Take the pan off the heat, add the cannellini beans and, using a potato masher, mash the beans up with the onion, leaving a few whole ones for texture. Allow to cool for a few minutes, then transfer to a mixing bowl and stir through the courgette, mozzarella, Parmesan, balsamic vinegar and basil. Season with plenty of black pepper and perhaps a little more salt. Taste to check the seasoning, it needs a rather generous hand. Crack in one of the eggs and stir really well to combine. You can make the fritter mixture ahead up to this point, and let it rest in the fridge.

When you are ready to eat, set yourself up a little production line on the worktop. Add the flour to a small bowl, beat the

second egg in another small bowl and spread out the breadcrumbs on a large plate. Take a generous tablespoonful of mixture, shape into a ball and dip into the flour, rolling around carefully to ensure an even coating. Then dip it into the egg and finally into the breadcrumbs, flattening it into a patty with the palm of your hand. Place on a clean plate, and repeat with the rest of the mixture. The uncooked fritters are a little fragile and need a gentle touch.

Heat a good centimetre or so of oil in a deep frying pan. When hot, carefully add the fritters and fry for 2–3 minutes until crisp and golden, then flip over with a fish slice and fry them on the other side. You may need to cook them in 2 batches. Drain on kitchen paper but be sure to eat them while piping hot and crisp.

15th July

American breakfast pancakes

ON A WET AND WINDY MORNING

The weekend often brings a cry for pancakes at breakfast time – a meal Daddy and the kids generally take charge of, happily leaving me in peace to drink coffee and read the newspaper.

Today we have family staying and the weather is unseasonably and unhelpfully foul – wet, windy and wild. There is simply no need to rush over breakfast. I chop up a few of the last peaches from the tree, along with some big wedges off the ripest, most perfect melon I have had for a long time. There are raspberries, strawberries and apricots too, a feast of colours, flavours and textures all lined up in bowls for people to help themselves. We linger in the kitchen, spooning fruit and maple syrup over pancake after pancake after pancake.

Enough for 4–6, depending on greed

300g self-raising flour

2 tsp caster sugar

A pinch of salt

450ml milk

3 eggs

50g butter, melted & cooled, plus extra for frying

To serve:
A selection of fruit, chopped into bite-size pieces

Maple syrup

In a large mixing bowl, stir together the flour, sugar and salt and make a large well in the middle. In a large jug, measure the milk, then beat in the eggs and melted butter until well mixed. Pour into the flour and, using a balloon whisk, beat until smooth. Pour back into the jug and leave to rest for 15 minutes.

Melt a little butter over a medium heat in a large, preferably non-stick, frying pan. Once hot, pour in generous tablespoons of the batter in rounds – you want the pancakes to be the size of a small saucer. I can get about 4 in my pan. Once the surface begins to bubble – they cook quickly, in less than a minute – flip them over and cook the other side for a few seconds. Transfer to a warmed plate, cover loosely with kitchen paper to keep warm and cook the remaining batter.

20th July

Saffron alioli

FOR A BOWL OF CREVETTES

Alioli, Catalan for 'garlic and oil', is the pungently garlicky Spanish mayonnaise often served with seafood. In this recipe I used saffron as well, to give both an earthy note and a fabulous colour. This sauce was made in honour of the shiny salmon-pink crevettes, giant cooked prawns, that were piled high on ice at the fishmonger's. Unable to resist, I came home with a vast sack for dinner. As is so often the way with me, a case of eyes bigger than belly.

Much like the crab and mayonnaise on page 81, this meal was a truly simple affair, mid-summer eating at its best. Just crevettes, alioli, bread, wine and a little salad, designed to be lingeringly sociable, effortless and a bit decadent.

I find with alioli, unlike with the classic mayonnaise, you can increase the proportion of strong extra virgin olive oil to flavourless sunflower. The pungency of the garlic seems to balance out any bitterness the olive oil can bring. This served four of us, with around 1.2kg crevettes to share.

Serves 4

Good pinch or 2 of saffron strands, plus 2 tbsp boiling water

2 egg yolks

Juice of ½–1 lemon

3 fat cloves garlic, crushed

Salt

150ml sunflower oil

150ml extra virgin olive oil

Freshly ground black pepper

Sprinkle the saffron into a heatproof glass and pour over the boiling water. Set aside to infuse.

In a freestanding food mixer, or a large mixing bowl if you are using an electric beater, whisk together the egg yolks with the juice of half a lemon. Add the garlic and a pinch of salt. Then begin to add the oil, drop by drop, whisking really well between each addition. Once the sauce has started to thicken and emulsify you can begin to add the oil a little faster, a few drops at a time, but take care not to go too fast.

Once all the oil is in, pour in the saffron plus its soaking water, season with black pepper and whisk again. Taste and add more lemon if it needs sharpening a little. If it is lemony enough but too thick in consistency, you can thin it a little by adding a splash of boiling water from the kettle.

23rd July

Pea, yellow courgette & mint quiche

ANOTHER DAY, ANOTHER COURGETTE

It is somewhat ironic that the vegetable I find the easiest to grow, the humble courgette, is among the blandest to eat. Don't get me wrong, I do like courgettes, but four plants seem to be yielding enough for every-day eating, which is not necessarily desirable. Next year I shall limit myself to two plants so I only have to eat them every other day. At least I chose to plant a yellow variety this year, Gold Rush, their vivid skin making them just a touch more exotic, even if they taste exactly the same. Peas, on the other hand, I can't get enough of, but sadly they are nearly over now, with the last bowlful of pods harvested for this summery quiche.

Serves 4

For the pastry:

200g plain flour

A pinch of salt

100g butter, diced

25g Parmesan, finely grated

3 tbsp cold water

1 egg white, for brushing

For the filling:

25g butter

200g courgette, thinly sliced

Approx.150g freshly podded peas (from a generous bowlful of pods) or frozen peas, defrosted

1 clove garlic, crushed

A generous handful of mint leaves, roughly chopped

2 eggs, plus 1 yolk (use the white for brushing the pastry)

150ml double cream

75ml milk

50g freshly grated Parmesan

Salt & freshly ground black pepper

Begin with the pastry, which I usually do in a food processor for speed. Pulse the flour and salt with the butter until you have a crumb-like texture, then add the Parmesan and pulse to mix. Add two-thirds of the water and pulse again for a few seconds until it forms a ball, adding the remaining water only if it looks dry. With a little patience and cool hands it can be satisfying to make the pastry by lightly rubbing the fat and flour together between finger and thumb. Whichever way you make it, the important thing is to let it rest, wrapped in clingfilm, in the fridge for at least 30 minutes before you use it. This allows the gluten in the flour to relax back to its pre-kneaded shape, giving you two benefits – you are less likely to get shrinkage on cooking (important when you need a substantial shell to hold the filling) and, secondly, the pastry will have a softer, more crumbly texture. Overworked and unrested pastry can be tough and chewy.

Preheat the oven to 190°C/Gas 5. Roll out the pastry and use it to line a 23–25cm loose-based tart tin. Prick the base all over with a fork and bake blind, lined with baking paper and beans, for 15 minutes until golden and crisp on the edges. Remove the paper and beans and brush all over with the egg white (for additional crispness), then return to the oven for a further 5 minutes to dry out. Turn the oven down to 170°C/Gas 3.

While the pastry is cooking, prepare the filling. Melt the butter over a low heat and sweat the courgette and peas with the garlic for a few minutes until they are soft but still with a little bite. Turn off the heat and stir through the mint.

In a small bowl beat together the eggs and egg yolk with the cream and milk. Stir through the Parmesan and season with salt and black pepper.

Spread the filling over the cooked tart case and gently pour over the custard mixture. Return to the oven and bake for 25 minutes or so until the filling is set and the top golden.

29th July

Gooseberry & elderflower clafoutis

Gooseberries are one of those things that are loved or loathed. Unfortunately if you adore them, and I do, they are pretty much impossible to buy in all but the best-stocked greengroceries. So the best way, if at all possible, is to find a little corner of the garden and plant your own bush. I like them so much that this spring saw me planting my second bush, a variety called Hinnomaki Red, chosen for its claret-coloured fruit and prolific nature. And prolific it certainly is. I wasn't expecting much of it this year, but barely two months after it went into the ground it yielded 375g of ripe fruit.

I used them to make a clafoutis, a French batter pudding studded with fresh fruit, traditionally cherries. I suppose you could consider it to be a sweetly dense version of toad-in-the-hole. The most fiddly part of this easy dessert is topping and tailing the gooseberries – a time-consuming but necessary job I find is best done sat at the table using a pair of sharp scissors.

Serves 4–6

3 eggs

75g butter, melted & cooled, plus a little for greasing the dish

225ml milk

75ml elderflower cordial

Finely grated zest of 1 lemon

90g caster sugar

75g plain flour

50g ground almonds

1 tsp baking powder

375g gooseberries, topped & tailed

75g granulated sugar

Icing sugar for dusting

Preheat the oven to 180°C/Gas 4.

In a mixing bowl, lightly whisk together the eggs, melted butter, milk, elderflower cordial and lemon zest. Sprinkle over the sugar and sift over the flour, ground almonds and baking powder and whisk together gently until you have a smooth lump-free batter. Set aside.

Take a baking dish that will fit the fruit in a single layer and grease the inside with a little butter. Tip in the gooseberries, scatter over the sugar and bake in the oven for 10 minutes, by which time the fruit should be soft. Pour over the batter and return to the oven for 25–30 minutes or until a skewer inserted comes out clean.

Serve, dusted with a little icing sugar, hot straight from the oven or allow to cool to room temperature.

31st July
Broad bean, feta & mint omelette

The broad bean plants have withered and wilted and I have finally admitted defeat to the millions, possibly even billions, of sticky black fly that have invaded them so vigorously. So out they come, and in their place I plant the little cavolo nero plants I have been nurturing in pots. I honestly don't know whether I will grow broad beans again next year. They looked tatty so readily, and the yield of pods was low. I always, always pod *and* skin my broad beans – I find them practically inedible otherwise – but once I'd done that all I had left were a couple of handfuls of bright green beans. Just enough to make a simple and delicious omelette with tangy feta and some roughly torn fresh mint.

One trick to a perfect omelette is a really hot frying pan, into which you toss a knob of unsalted butter and a drizzle of olive oil. As soon as the butter is foaming, pour in the seasoned beaten egg, 2 or 3 depending on hunger. If the pan is hot enough the egg should

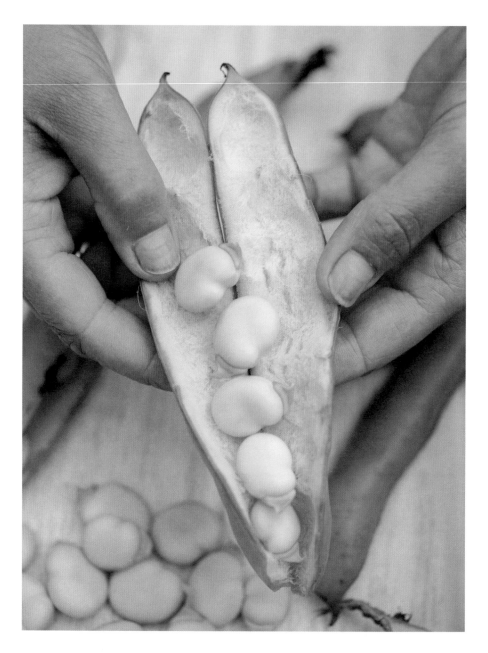

seal in an instant. Use a fork to draw the sides into the middle, and give the pan a swirl to encourage the uncooked egg to the sides. The whole process should take less than a minute. Once it has nearly set, crumble over some feta, add cooked, skinned broad beans and sprinkle with freshly chopped mint before folding over.

The second secret to an omelette is to eat it almost as quickly as it was made. So before you even think about adding the egg to the pan, be ready with your filling, your plate, your fork and your glass of wine. A good omelette is a fine thing indeed that deserves you to be ready to receive it, no last-minute faffing around allowed. Of course, that means omelettes are best reserved for solitary dining, or dining in pairs at most. Which to my mind is no bad thing at all.

2nd August

Red pepper & goat's cheese tart

I first ate a tart similar to this many moons ago at university in Manchester. Someone, sadly I don't remember who, had made a tart packed full of red peppers and tomatoes that tasted utterly summery and Mediterranean. I have been making a variation of it ever since, though over time I have tinkered and twiddled with the recipe, sometimes adding a few anchovies, sometimes a generous handful of torn basil leaves. But here is my very favourite rendition.

You could use ready-made pastry to line your tin, as indeed I do when I am short of time and patience, but the beauty of making your own lies in the extra flavours you can add – a sprinkle of dried herbs, a pinch of chilli powder, a good grind of black pepper, or a liberal grating of freshly grated Parmesan. I had six to feed for supper so I chose a large rectangular tin, about 35 x 25cm, but a large round quiche tin would do just as well. Whatever shape you go for, do make sure it is metal – cooking pastry in ceramic or glass is never a great success. If your tin does not have a loose base, line it with a couple of long, wide strips of baking paper to help you lift the cooked tart out. We ate this with new potatoes and salad.

Serves 6

For the pastry:
250g plain flour, plus extra for dusting

125g butter, cut into 1cm cubes

1–2 tsp dried herbs

Salt & freshly ground black pepper

4–6 tbsp very cold water

For the filling:
3 tbsp olive oil

4 large red peppers, deseeded & chopped

4 cloves garlic, crushed

3 x 400g tins chopped tomatoes

1 tsp granulated sugar

3 tbsp capers, roughly chopped

Salt & freshly ground black pepper

4 eggs, lightly beaten

200g goat's cheese, cut into 5mm-thick slices

Make the pastry by putting the flour and butter into the bowl of a food processor. Pulse for a few seconds at a time until the butter and flour resemble coarse flaky breadcrumbs. Do not over-mix or the pastry will toughen. Add the dried herbs, season generously and pulse again until just mixed. Then add 4 tablespoons of the water and pulse until it starts to clump together, adding more water if required. Tip the pastry crumbs on to a sheet of clingfilm, draw up the sides and press into a rough ball. Wrap tightly and chill for at least 30 minutes.

Preheat the oven to 180°C/Gas 4. Lightly dust the worktop with flour and roll out the pastry to fit the tin you have chosen, pressing it well into the corners. Prick the base all over with a fork and line with a sheet of baking paper and baking beans.

Bake blind for 20 minutes, then remove the paper and beans and return to the oven for a further 5 minutes to dry the base out.

While the pastry is cooking, begin the filling. Heat the oil in a large saucepan until it is really hot. Add the peppers and fry over a high heat for around 15–20 minutes, stirring every now and then, until they start to caramelize at the edges. Be brave – a little colour, even slight charring here and there, will add loads of flavour to the peppers. Add the garlic and fry for just a few seconds before pouring in the tomatoes. Stir in the sugar and reduce the heat a little. Simmer for around 20 minutes until the sauce has a thick and almost jam-like consistency. Remove from the heat, stir in the capers and season to taste. Allow to cool a little before stirring the beaten egg into the peppers.

Pour into the cooked pastry case and arrange the goat's cheese on top, grinding a little extra black pepper over the slices. Bake for 30–35 minutes until the filling has just set and the cheese is melting and golden. Remove from the oven and allow to cool a little before serving in thick wedges.

5th August

Lemon cheesecake with raspberries

I adore a proper home-made cheesecake. Its creamy, velvety texture is a true indulgence on so many levels. You need time and patience for the baking and the chilling, and your wallet need not be too slight either – with all that cheese, cream and fresh fruit, this is far from the cheap throw-it-together puddings I make on a more regular basis. And as for what the health police would have to say

… I prefer not to think about it. But what a glorious treat it is, and once in a while what a true pleasure both to make and to eat. On this occasion I was inspired by the glut of cheap raspberries in the shops, but any seasonal fruit would be lovely: strawberries, blackberries, blueberries – whatever feels right.

As a small aside, I used the leftover lemon, cut in half, to shove inside a chicken I was roasting that evening – the best strategy I know for ensuring a fragrant and moist bird. I have no plans to give up eating chicken, but watching the hens in the garden as I do, this gives me a new level of respect for these gorgeous feathery creatures, and I now always (without fail) ensure I buy a free-range bird.

As for the tin, I would normally make a cheesecake in a round springform one. But on this occasion I chose a rectangular loaf tin, simply because I fancied the idea of cutting a neat square slice.

Serves 6

For the biscuit base:
175g digestive biscuits
45g butter, melted

2 large eggs, plus 1 yolk
150g caster sugar
Finely grated zest of 1 lemon

For the cheesecake:
600g full-fat cream cheese
125g full-fat crème fraîche

For the raspberry topping:
300g fresh raspberries
1 tbsp icing sugar

Preheat the oven to 160°C/Gas 3. Then prepare the tin – either a 25cm springform tin or a long loaf tin of about 30cm. Line the base with baking paper, and butter well on the sides. With my loaf tin I cut a long strip that came up the ends to help lift the cake out.

Whizz the biscuits in a food processor until they form fine crumbs, then pour in the melted butter and pulse until thoroughly mixed. Tip into the tin and press down firmly with the back of a metal spoon. Chill in the fridge while you make the rest.

In a clean food processor, or in a bowl with a wooden spoon, beat together the cream cheese, crème fraîche, eggs and egg yolk. When they are really smooth, stir in the sugar and lemon zest.

Take the tin out of the fridge and wrap the base and sides in a double layer of foil, then lower into a large roasting tray. Pour the cream cheese mixture over the biscuit base and level a little with the flat of a knife. Add enough boiling water to the roasting tray so it comes just over halfway up the side of the cheesecake tin. Cooking in a water bath creates a gentle and nurturing heat, resulting in a really smooth-textured cheesecake.

Carefully transfer the roasting tray to the oven and cook for 45 minutes. Then turn off the oven and let it cool, with the door shut, for 30 minutes. Lift the tin out of the roasting tray, unwrap the foil and place on a cooling rack. When it has reached room temperature, transfer to the fridge to chill for at least 4 hours.

Slide a knife round the tin to loosen the edges, and ease out the cake. Transfer to a serving plate and scatter with about two-thirds of the raspberries. Purée the remaining raspberries with a little icing sugar to make a quick coulis and drizzle over the top.

11th August

Salt & pepper scotch eggs, and falafel eggs, a vegetarian alternative

I love scotch eggs – even the over-chilled ones bought in haste in garage forecourts are something of a guilty pleasure to break up long car journeys – but home-made ones are pretty phenomenal and well worth making occasionally. Today's version had a crisp

breadcrumb coating spiked with plenty of flaky sea salt and coarsely ground black peppercorns. I used thick herby sausages, which I skinned, instead of plain sausagemeat, as they tend to have more flavour.

Buoyed by their success, I decided to try a meat-free version. For this my eggs were wrapped not in pork but a tasty falafel mixture – a Middle-Eastern spiced chickpea purée. The coating is not quite as robust as sausagemeat and so it's even more important to give them a double dip in the breadcrumbs – it is this shell that protects the chickpea purée and stops it from disintegrating on frying. I found a shorter cooking time combined with a slightly higher temperature helped as well. The result was a picnic feast of savoury eggs suitable for vegetarians and carnivores alike.

For both these recipes I picked smaller eggs, as once they are wrapped up in their coating they end up a good size. If you use large eggs you may need to make the coating a touch thinner in order to cover them.

Salt & pepper scotch eggs

Makes 4

6 eggs, size small to medium

400g sausagemeat

120g fresh breadcrumbs

2 tsp black peppercorns, crushed

1 tsp sea salt flakes

Vegetable oil for deep-frying

Place 4 of the eggs in a small pan and cover with cold water. Bring steadily up to the boil, reduce the heat to a simmer and cook for 5 minutes. Remove from the heat and run under cold water until cool. Peel and set aside. Crack the other 2 eggs into a small bowl and lightly beat.

Divide the sausagemeat into 4 balls, pressing each one flat

between the palms of your hands. Put one of the eggs into the centre and fold and press the meat around it so it is completely covered.

Put the breadcrumbs into a wide shallow bowl and mix in the crushed peppercorns and salt.

Dip each of the sausage-covered eggs in the beaten egg, then roll in the crumbs. Once all 4 eggs have a coat of crumbs, repeat the dipping and rolling to give them a second coat of crumbs.

Heat the oil in a deep-fat fryer to 170°C and cook the eggs for 7 minutes. Serve hot or cold.

Falafel eggs

Makes 4

6 eggs, size small to medium

1 small onion, finely chopped

2 tbsp olive oil

2 cloves garlic, chopped

1 tsp dried chilli flakes

2 tsp cumin seeds, roughly ground

2 tsp coriander seeds, roughly ground

1 x 400g tin chickpeas, drained & rinsed

1 tbsp tahini paste

A small bunch coriander, chopped

Salt & freshly ground black pepper

120g fresh breadcrumbs

Vegetable oil for deep-frying

As with the scotch eggs, cook 4 of the eggs, run under cold water, peel and set aside. Lightly beat the remaining 2 eggs in a small bowl.

Set a small frying pan over a low heat and sweat the onion in the olive oil for 10 minutes until it is beginning to soften and turn translucent. Add the garlic and spices and fry for a further minute. Remove from the heat and tip into a food processor, along with the chickpeas, tahini and coriander. Season well with salt and black pepper and whizz to a smooth thick paste. You need the mixture to be firm, but if it's too stiff to process, add a little more tahini to loosen it a little. Scrape into a bowl and chill in the fridge for an hour or so to firm up.

Divide into 4 balls and flatten each between the palms of your hands. Place an egg in the centre and fold and press the falafel coating around the egg so it is completely covered. Dip each wrapped egg in turn in the beaten egg, then roll in the breadcrumbs. Once again, repeat the dipping and rolling process to give each a double coating of breadcrumbs.

Heat the oil in a deep-fat fryer to 180°C and cook for 5–6 minutes until crisp and golden.

16th August

Baked rice pudding with greengages

Delicious though they are, greengages, like gooseberries, are a rarity in the shops. When perfectly ripe their sweet melting flesh is a wonder, making the most delicious crumbles, pies and puddings you could imagine. Unfortunately my precious greengage tree, after four years of generous fruiting, decided to die without any visible or obvious reason. A complete, not to say rather expensive, gardening failure. I have planted another and look forward to fruit in the future, but in the meantime I snatch them up if I see them in the greengrocer's. In this recipe they are baked with a rich creamy rice pudding, which I think tastes best eaten at room temperature.

Serves 4–6

120g short-grain rice (traditional pudding rice or arborio risotto rice)

775ml full-fat milk

125ml double cream

1 vanilla pod, split lengthways

50g butter, plus a little extra for greasing the dish

75g caster sugar

2 eggs, beaten

300g greengages, cut in half, stone removed

3 tbsp Demerara sugar

Put the rice, milk, cream and vanilla pod in a saucepan and bring up to a gentle simmer. Turn the heat to a minimum and cook for 15–20 minutes, stirring from time to time, until the rice is just tender. Add the butter and caster sugar and stir until they have melted and dissolved. Turn off the heat and cool for 10 minutes.

Preheat the oven to 160°C/Gas 3.

Remove the vanilla pod, scraping out the seeds and stirring them through the rice. Add the beaten egg, stir, then pour into a greased baking dish. Arrange the greengages, cut-side down, over the pudding. Sprinkle the Demerara sugar over the top.

Bake in the oven for about 50–55 minutes until just set with a lovely light golden crust. As the pudding cools it will thicken.

20th August

A simple Russian salad

Russian salad – potato salad with extra bits – is ubiquitous in Spanish tapas bars. There seems to be much debate as to why exactly it is 'Russian' but one thing for certain is that every bar has its own variation. They can contain peas, carrots, tuna or even bits of jamón. Mine contains none of these and was devised purely to showcase

my home-grown beetroot and French beans. Sadly, upon pulling up my beets, all I found underneath the lush, purple-tinged leaves were thin, straggly roots. A vegetable-growing disaster sending me straight back to the beetroot drawing board for next year. Instead I used a couple of fine specimens from the greengrocer's.

I generally use a good quality, ready-made mayo for any sort of potato salad, but you could, of course, always make your own (see page 81). If you are preparing this ahead, you may want to leave out the beetroot until just before you serve as it has a tendency to bleed its colour – which I quite like, but it's up to you.

Serves 4

300g raw beetroot – about 2–3 medium

600g waxy salad potatoes

150g green beans, cut into 1cm pieces

2 eggs, hard-boiled

For the dressing:

3 tbsp crème fraîche

3 tbsp mayonnaise

1 tbsp capers, roughly chopped

1 clove garlic, crushed

Juice of ½–1 lemon

Salt & freshly ground black pepper

Small bunch of parsley, chopped

Making this salad is simply a game of boiling, peeling and chopping. Cut the leaves off the beetroot, leaving a 3cm stalk, and wash them gently under running water. Take care not to pierce or damage the skin or root or they will 'bleed' when you boil them. Place in a large pan and generously cover with cold water. Bring up to the boil, turn down the heat and simmer for an hour or so until tender. They may take a little more or less depending on how big they are – top up with extra boiling water if you need to. Once they are tender, drain and allow to cool. When cool enough to handle, peel and dice into 1cm cubes, wearing gloves if you are at all bothered by pink fingers.

Put the potatoes in a pan of cold, lightly salted water and bring to the boil. Reduce the heat and cook until tender, about 10–15 minutes depending on size. Drain and cool slightly before peeling and dicing into 1cm cubes. Set aside to cool.

In another pan plunge the green beans into boiling water and cook until they are just tender, about 4–5 minutes. Drain and run under cold water to cool quickly. Set aside.

Peel the hard-boiled eggs, rinsing under cold water to remove any little bits of shell, then chop into roughly 1cm pieces.

Make the dressing in a large roomy bowl by mixing the crème fraîche, mayonnaise, capers and garlic. Season to taste with lemon juice, salt and black pepper and stir through most of the parsley, reserving a little to garnish. Add all the chopped vegetables to the dressing and fold gently to mix. Spoon into a serving bowl, and scatter the chopped egg and a sprinkling of parsley over.

26th August

Blackberry & apple parfait with maple oat crumbs

Maybe it's just a hazy memory, but blackberries for me signify the very first whiff of early autumn, of going back to school tanned, windswept and full of tales of summer holiday adventures. I remember being desperate for the weather to turn chilly so I could proudly show off a new coat, somewhat ironic after a summer spent wishing it would be just a little warmer and sunnier. These days blackberries seem to appear earlier and earlier, and by August they are often in full swing in the hedgerows, making picking them more of a summer holiday activity.

The inspiration for this pudding comes from the wonderful Claudia Roden's book *The Food of Spain*. In it she has a recipe for

'apple cream', a traditional dessert hailing from Asturias in northern Spain, which incidentally is where my father now lives. Being frozen, my dish is really rather different, but does contain the apples, the eggs and the cream, along with plenty of blackberries that give it the most wonderful magenta colour. A nod to the inevitable autumn puddings of the coming months, the crispy oat sprinkles are slightly suggestive of crumble and add a pleasing buttery crunch. This recipe serves a generous 8, but it will keep happily in the freezer, well wrapped up, for 2–3 weeks.

Serves 8

200g caster sugar
3 tbsp cold water
900g Bramley apples
300g blackberries
300ml double cream
Juice of 1 lemon
3 eggs

For the maple oat crumbs:
100g oats
75ml maple syrup
50g butter, melted
1 tsp vanilla extract

Put the sugar and water in a heavy-based saucepan. Set over a low heat and stir until the sugar dissolves. Peel and core the apples, cutting into 1cm cubes and dropping them into the hot sugar syrup as you go. Adding the cut apple to the hot syrup reduces the amount of discolouring you get from oxidization. Once all the apple is added, stir well to coat and cover with a lid. Simmer over a low heat for about 20 minutes until the apple is soft. Every now and then, lift the lid and mash with the back of a wooden spoon to break it up. Add the blackberries, re-cover and cook for a further 5 minutes until they are soft.

Remove from the heat and stir through the cream and lemon juice. Separate the eggs, adding the whites to a large mixing bowl. Stir the yolks through the fruit, mixing well until completely combined, and set aside to cool. Transferring from the hot pan to a shallow dish will speed up the cooling process.

Whip up the egg whites with a balloon whisk until they form soft fluffy peaks. Using a large metal spoon and a figure-of-eight motion, fold the egg white through the cool creamy fruit.

Line a large loaf tin (approximately 30 x 10 x 6cm) with a double layer (for security) of clingfilm. Pour in the mixture and level with a knife. Cover the top with another layer of clingfilm, followed by a snug layer of tin foil. Set in the freezer for at least 6 hours, or overnight, until firm.

To make the maple oat crumbs, mix all the ingredients in a bowl and spread on a baking tray. Bake in the oven at 160°C/Gas 3 for 25–30 minutes until golden brown. Remove from the oven to cool and crisp up, then break into little clumps.

To serve, remove the parfait from the freezer half an hour or so before you want to eat to allow it to soften a little. Invert on to a serving plate and peel off the clingfilm. Scatter a few crumbs over the top and pass the rest around in a bowl.

27th August

Curried egg mayonnaise

Egg mayonnaise is the most quintessentially British of sandwich fillings, loved in hazy-day summer picnics and loathed in school packed lunches, the gaseous smell a source of acute childhood embarrassment. My mum's favourite way with it was to stir through a generous pinch of curry power. These days I like to mix up my own spices fresh so that I can adjust the balance of flavours to my liking. Either way, eggs and spices have a natural affinity. If you are using whole dry spices, it really is worthwhile toasting them in a hot frying pan for a few seconds. It wakes up the flavour no end.

I think one to one and a half eggs per person is about right for a

well-filled sandwich. On a picnic I prefer to pile my egg mayo into a bowl alongside a stack of bread and let people construct their own sarnies – I have far too much sandwich-making in my life with the weekday packed lunches. I didn't eat mine with bread at all but dolloped it on top of a pile of peppery watercress, and delicious it was too.

For each mashed hard-boiled egg, allow:

A pinch of each of the following: dried chilli flakes, cumin seeds, mustard seeds, paprika & garam masala

A dollop of mayo

Salt & freshly ground black pepper

Put the spices in a small frying pan and toast for a minute or so over a medium heat. As soon as you can smell their aroma, tip into a pestle and mortar and grind roughly. Sprinkle over the mashed-up hard-boiled egg, mix in the mayonnaise and season with salt and black pepper.

30th August

Chocolate-dipped nougat with candied orange, honey & almonds

Tomorrow is my tenth wedding anniversary and I find myself wondering where the years have flown. Then I look about me: two gorgeous, bright, strong-willed children, a larger than sensible collection of animals and a lot of fun memories. Not to mention damned hard work and the usual blood, sweat, tears and plate-juggling that comes from keeping it all together. All in all, we've

done well and that has to be worth celebrating. Ten years is, apparently, a 'tin' anniversary – not instantly glamorous that one, is it? But what about some delicious home-made treats all packaged up in a suitably manly tin box? He has a sweet tooth, my man, and I know this will go down a storm.

For all its teeth-wrecking possibilities, I love nougat, but have never thought of making my own until now. I won't pretend it was instant or particularly easy, but as a special gift for a loved one it's a good thing to stretch oneself occasionally, I think. A sugar thermometer will make life infinitely easier – the setting of the nougat relies on the sugar being boiled to a specific temperature, known in sweet-making as the 'hard crack stage'. A freestanding food mixer is also pretty much essential as the mix needs to be beaten hard and fast as it cools.

If you are making the candied orange yourself, you need to add another good hour or so to the time it takes to prepare this confection, but I urge you to do so – it will far exceed anything you can buy. The recipe below makes twice as much as you need for the nougat, but it will keep for several weeks in a box in the fridge, and it's a great addition to home-made cakes or for general nibbling.

Makes about 40 small squares

For the candied orange:
4 oranges
150g granulated sugar

For the nougat:
200g whole blanched almonds
2 egg whites
500g granulated sugar

250g honey
100ml cold water
1 tbsp orange flower water
1 tsp vanilla extract
50g candied orange peel, chopped
100g dark chocolate, broken into pieces

To make the candied orange, score through the peel of each orange to remove it, ideally in quarters. Lay each quarter on its back on a chopping board and use a sharp knife to shave off as much white pith as you can. Cut the peel into long strips of 5mm thick and put in a heavy-based saucepan. Cover with plenty of cold water, bring up to the boil and boil for a couple of minutes. Drain, rinse and repeat.

After boiling the peel twice, return it to the pan, this time with 250ml cold water and the sugar. Bring up to the boil and cook for 15 minutes, until the peel is soft and yields easily to the point of a sharp knife. Drain, reserving the syrup if you like – it would be good to add to citrusy cocktails or pour over a sponge cake – and spread the peel out in a single layer on a baking tray. Bake in a warm oven at 140°C/Gas 2 for about 30 minutes until dry, turning halfway to make sure they 'cook' evenly. Remove, chop into smaller pieces and set aside while you make the nougat.

Begin by toasting the almonds. Turn the oven up to 160°C/Gas 3. Spread the almonds out on a baking tray and toast in the oven for 10 or so minutes until they are golden brown. Set aside.

Tip the egg whites into the squeaky-clean bowl of a freestanding food mixer and, using the whisk attachment, whisk until they are stiff. Turn off the mixer.

Put the sugar, honey and cold water into a large heavy-based saucepan. Set over a low heat and stir until the sugar has dissolved. Then prop a sugar thermometer in the pan and increase the heat to medium high. You need to boil the sugar and honey syrup, without stirring, until it reaches 148°C, the hard crack stage. This will take a good 10–15 minutes. Take care that it doesn't boil over – if it looks like it's about to, reduce the heat and continue boiling. Once the volume has reduced a little, turn it back up again but keep an eagle eye on it.

When the sugar and honey syrup has almost reached temperature, say 140°C, turn the mixer back on and continue whisking the egg white on a medium-high speed. When the syrup has reached 148°C, remove the thermometer and set aside on a plate to cool down slowly. With the motor running, and using a great deal of care, slowly pour the boiling syrup into the egg white in a thin steady trickle. Once all the syrup is in, add the orange flower water and vanilla, turn the mixer up to full speed and beat for 10 minutes. At this stage the mixture should be stiff and exceptionally sticky. If it is not thick and stiff, beat for a further couple of minutes. Reduce the speed a little, add the toasted almonds and the chopped candied orange peel, and beat once more until evenly combined.

Grease and line a 23cm square tin with baking paper. Scrape the mixture into the tin and level as best you can with the flat of a table knife. Keep wetting the knife to make this job easier. To achieve a smooth surface, wet the palm of your hand and use this for a final touch. Set the nougat aside for several hours or overnight until really firm. Turn on to a board and chop into small pieces with a large sharp knife.

Melt the chocolate in a small heatproof bowl set over a pan of barely simmering water. Using a spoon, drizzle the chocolate over the surface of the nougat, then set aside to dry and harden on a cooling rack.

Autumn
Preparing for hibernation

Early autumn is a season of plenty, when the garden yields up its full bounty, while the nip in the air dictates a certain flexibility to our cooking. Al fresco summery salads one day, warming bowls of stew the next. I adore autumn and have an almost childlike nostalgia for its rituals – the buzz of going back to school with a brand new pencil case, squeezing luminous icing on scary cupcakes for Halloween, swirling apples in molten toffee for Bonfire Night, crunching through the first of the fallen leaves. It is also a time when we are drawn inwards to a feeling of 'home', of preparing ourselves and our families for the long winter months ahead, and our cooking turns naturally towards warmth and comfort.

If any season has a smell, it's autumn. The garden becomes the scene of a slow, quiet decay. I don't particularly enjoy looking at it but I do adore the earthy, woody scent that it brings. Our north-facing plot is still offering us up many edible goodies. There are pumpkins a-plenty and more courgettes than I know what to do with. The cherry tomatoes have at long last ripened, as have the Muscat grapes that drip sweetly off the vine. One day I will get round to making the wine I always intended them for. In the meantime, the chickens love them, not caring about the pips that make them virtually inedible as fruit. This is the time of year when I am content to let the hens roam free for long periods, happy that they are doing some of the necessary autumn clear-up for me. They eagerly hoover up the grapes that have fallen, and there are rich invertebrate pickings to be had under the ever-growing piles of damp fallen leaves. They eat and forage with such conviction that you get the sense they are fattening themselves up for the coming winter months.

September

Salami, pesto & ricotta frittata
Autumn apple & walnut cake
Cheese & tomato scrambled egg
Courgette & lime muffins
Cheddar & wholegrain mustard
croquetas
Mojito sorbet
Plum, amaretto & almond crumble
with proper vanilla custard
Caramelized onion, Cheddar
& rosemary scone bread
Italian pear & ginger baked cheesecake

October

Sage tagliatelle with roast pumpkin
& Stilton
Bacon, parsnip & cheese brunch
muffins
Cauliflower bhajis with raita
Quick and simple sponge recipe to
make two birthday cakes
Spanish flan
Chakchouka with merguez sausages
& baked eggs
Warm brioche
Carrot & cumin tart
Coconut marshmallows

November

Baked eggs with wild mushrooms
& cream
Toffee-apple & jam doughnuts
Quince, Marsala & lemon trifle
Two unconventional moussakas
Korean egg toast
Far Breton with Armagnac prunes
Smoked haddock chowder with
poached eggs

I too get the feeling I am fuelling my body with extra sustenance at this time of year and food is often at the forefront of my mind. As the days shorten and the dampness sets in, I happily shut myself away for hours in the kitchen, making chutneys and pickles, filling pies with luscious autumn fruit, baking sweet treats for the weekend, taking the time to make fresh pasta or batch-cooking soups and stews for the freezer. These are things I wouldn't dream of doing mid-summer but getting back to the slower, gentler ways of cooking, finding quiet afternoons to make things from scratch and stir and simmer over time, seems to be one of the things autumn was made for. Once you take away the pressure of simply having to put something on the table to feed hungry mouths, the process of cooking instantly becomes more pleasurable. I find myself more relaxed about letting the children get stuck in with kneading dough or shaping biscuits, not minding so much about the mess, muddle and chaos that invariably comes from letting them take charge.

But I am also mindful of how important it is to snatch at any opportunity to enjoy the fresh air, sunny days becoming few and far between. The dogs need walking whatever the weather, and the kids are encouraged to play outside, wrapped in an extra layer or two. On mild afternoons we sometimes picnic at the very top of the garden where the sun still casts a little warmth.

Autumn recipes are about being happy to spend all afternoon pottering around a deliciously scented steam-filled kitchen . . .

2nd September

Salami, pesto & ricotta frittata

AN ODDS-AND-ENDS PICNIC LUNCH

To me, a frittata is simply an Italian version of a Spanish omelette, with a few extra ingredients thrown in. Unlike a tortilla (see page 96), I tend not to turn a frittata in the pan but to set the top under a hot grill, which allows me to melt some cheese on the surface too. They are wonderfully useful things to make, great for using up odds and sods in the fridge, and you can add whatever you fancy – a few slices of roast pepper or courgettes, bits of ham or smoked fish, leftover ends of cheese. This version was a combination of half a pack of salami and a little leftover ricotta cheese. A thick wedge is the perfect thing to take on a picnic, which was what I had planned to do with this one. The reality was that it rained, again, and as we ate it inside I found myself wistfully wondering if we had missed our last chance for al fresco eating this year.

I urge you to make your own pesto. The ingredients are simply chucked in a food processor. It takes only a few minutes, but the taste difference between home-made and the shop stuff is unfathomable. I often make a quick batch with the kids. They love it for their tea. The recipe below will make about twice what you need for the frittata, and it will keep, covered in a layer of oil, for a few days in the fridge.

Makes 1 small frittata, enough for 2 for lunch or 4 as part of a picnic spread

For the pesto:

A large bunch of fresh basil, tough stalk ends removed

3–4 tbsp extra virgin olive oil

3 tbsp pine nuts

1 clove garlic, crushed

15g Parmesan cheese, finely grated

Squeeze of lemon juice

Salt & freshly ground black pepper

For the frittata:

1 tbsp olive oil

1 small onion, finely sliced

1 clove garlic, crushed

A handful of frozen peas

6 eggs, lightly beaten and seasoned

6 slices of salami – I like finocchiona, which is flavoured with fennel seeds

6 tsp ricotta, about 75g

6 tsp pesto

To make the pesto, roughly tear up the bunch of basil and add to a food processor along with the oil. Process until you have a rough paste. Dry-fry the pine nuts in a small pan until they have toasted a nutty golden brown, then tip into the processor along with the garlic and Parmesan and whizz together. Finally season to taste with a little lemon juice, salt and black pepper.

In a small (about 20cm diameter) frying pan, preferably non-stick, heat the oil and fry the onion over a low heat for 10 minutes or so until softened and lightly caramelized. Add the garlic and the peas and fry for a further couple of minutes.

Pour in the seasoned egg and stir gently until it just begins to thicken and set. Fold each slice of salami into quarters and tuck gently into and under the surface of the frittata. Then dot over spoonfuls of ricotta and pesto, also pushing it under a little here and there.

Allow the frittata to cook gently over a low heat until it is set two-thirds of the way through, then slide the pan under a hot grill for a few minutes to finish cooking the surface.

9th September

Autumn apple & walnut cake

We have an apple tree in the garden that is gnarled, old and overgrown. It's in such dire need of a prune that I don't know where to start. Its branches twist and turn high over the roof of the outhouse and the fruit are impossible to reach. So we simply wait for them to fall, which they do regularly and with surprising velocity at this time of year. Every now and then we gather them up into whatever vessel is handy (today it was a plastic sandcastle bucket I'd just rescued from the new puppy) and take them inside to sort, peel, cut the bruises off and cook with. I have no idea what variety of apple they are – some sort of small sharp cooker. What I do know is that they make great crumbles, pies and cakes. So here is today's windfall recipe, a lightly spiced cake that is wonderful served warm. Your kitchen will smell phenomenal when it's baking: spicy, sweet and homely. This could indeed be the perfect thing to bake if you are trying to sell your house – no one will be able to resist such a domestic heaven!

Serves 6–8

150g butter, plus extra for greasing

150g light brown sugar

3 eggs

150g plain flour

50g oats

3 tsp baking powder

2 tsp ground cinnamon

200g chopped apple

80g walnuts, roughly chopped

Icing sugar mixed with a little ground cinnamon for dusting (optional)

Preheat the oven to 180°C/Gas 4. Line a springform cake tin of about 23–25cm with baking paper and grease with butter.

In a food mixer, or with an electric whisk, cream together the butter and sugar until light and fluffy. Add the eggs, one at a time,

beating well between each addition.

In a separate bowl mix together the flour, oats, baking powder and cinnamon. Stir through the chopped apple and walnuts so that each piece gets a floury coating. I always toss fruit for cakes through the flour to coat them – I seem to remember reading something in my dim and distant past that said it was supposed to prevent the fruit sinking. It seems to work, most of the time, so it's a habit I am happy to pass on.

Tip the dry ingredients into the sugar, butter and egg mixture, and fold until just combined. Pour into the prepared cake tin and bake for around 40 minutes or until a skewer inserted into the centre comes out clean.

Remove from the oven, ease from the tin and allow to cool a little before tucking in. I sprinkled the top with a little icing sugar and extra cinnamon – it looked pretty and gave an additional hit of aromatic spice.

14th September

Cheese & tomato scrambled egg

A HEARTY BREAKFAST FOR A HUNGRY DAY

I am not normally a breakfast person. My only true necessity first thing is a bucket of strong coffee. In contrast, my husband can devour four Weetabix in a single (and indeed brief) sitting. But just occasionally I feel ravenous in the morning. Today proceeded in its usual chaotic, flying-by-the-seat-of-my-pants fashion – two kids fed and watered, two packed lunches, a bit of shouting to get a move on, cleaning up after the not-quite-toilet-trained puppy – and once I returned home from the school run I found my thoughts greedily turning to food. Inspiration came from the bowl of shiny super-ripe pomodorino tomatoes sitting on the worktop. It is the perfect time of year for tomatoes, ripened sweetly over a long period. I think they are at their most delicious in September. Rather guiltily I whipped myself up a breakfast of cheese and tomato scrambled egg and quickly ate them with a thick slice of toasted rye bread. It absolutely hit the spot and kept me going for hours in a way that a bowl of cereal never could. I shall eat eggs for breakfast more often. This quantity serves one but can be easily multiplied up.

Serves 1

A knob of unsalted butter

5 ripe pomodorino tomatoes (any cherry variety or baby plum tomato would be good too), sliced in half

2 eggs, lightly beaten, seasoned generously with salt & freshly ground black pepper

Small wedge of mature Cheddar (about 40g), grated

A thick slice of toast – ideally wholemeal, granary or rye

Melt the butter gently in a small heavy-based saucepan and sauté the tomatoes for a minute or two until they just begin to soften. Pour in the seasoned egg, add the grated cheese and continue to cook, stirring from time to time, until creamy and just set. Eat immediately – so hungry was I that I devoured the lot standing at the kitchen worktop.

17th September

Courgette & lime muffins

The courgettes keep on coming and so out of necessity we keep on cooking with them. I am getting to the point of saturation. But today we have at least a change of scene with a batch of sweet lime-scented muffins, the recipe inspired by, and adapted from, the courgette cake in Nigella's baking bible, *How to Be a Domestic Goddess*. Not being a fan of thick, gloopy icing I opted for a sharper, tarter glaze to enhance the limey zing. And, just in case you were wondering, no, my kids wouldn't eat them. They never have been fans of the hiding-your-veg method of feeding your family, much preferring to see exactly what is on their plates. Still, all the more for us.

Makes 12

300g courgettes, yellow or green (about 3 medium-sized)

2 eggs

125ml vegetable oil

150g golden caster sugar

225g self-raising flour

½ tsp bicarbonate of soda

½ tsp baking powder

Juice & zest of 1 lime

For the lime drizzle icing:

100g icing sugar

Juice & finely grated zest of 2 limes

Preheat the oven to 180°C/Gas 4. Line a 12-hole muffin tin with paper cases.

Grate the courgettes and leave them for 30 minutes in a sieve suspended over a bowl to drain away their excess moisture. Weigh them down to help squeeze the water out; a small plate with a tin of beans on top will do the job.

In a large mixing bowl, beat the eggs, vegetable oil and sugar until well mixed and slightly fluffy. An electric whisk will make this easier, or use a food mixer. Sift in the flour, bicarbonate of soda and baking powder and beat well together. Finally, add the drained courgette and the lime juice and zest. Divide the mixture between the 12 muffin cases.

Bake for 20–25 minutes or until the muffins are golden brown and firm to the touch. Allow to cool completely on a wire rack before icing.

Make the icing by beating together the icing sugar with the lime juice and most of the zest until smooth. Drizzle the icing over the muffins, and decorate each with a little sprinkle of the remaining lime zest.

23rd September

Cheddar & wholegrain mustard croquetas

Tomorrow sees the second of my supper clubs, this one planned as a luscious early autumn feast of fruit, cheese and meat. I am expecting eighteen guests and there is much to be done. Today preparation has begun in earnest. I adore the Spanish jamón croquetas and wanted to try an anglicized version. Anything crisply fried and deeply savoury is a big hit in my book. These croquetas, I'm pleased to report, worked like a dream. Rich and super cheesy thanks to extra strong Cheddar, and packed with plenty of mustard punch. They are great served with a peppery watercress or rocket salad.

As an added bonus they freeze really well: just spread out on a baking tray and freeze solid before packing them into a box. They will take just a few minutes extra when cooked from frozen and make a gorgeous, indulgent supper for nights when you not only want to eat well but eat quickly too.

Makes 28–30, enough for 4–6 generous helpings

800ml milk

1 small onion, peeled and cut
into quarters

1 tsp whole black peppercorns

2 sprigs of rosemary

100g butter

150g plain flour

200g extra mature Cheddar,
grated

2 tbsp wholegrain mustard

2 eggs, beaten

200g fine dried breadcrumbs

Vegetable oil for deep-frying

In a heavy-based pan, bring the milk to the boil along with the onion, peppercorns and rosemary. Reduce the heat to as low as possible and simmer gently for 15 minutes to allow the flavours to infuse.

In a saucepan, melt the butter, then add the flour and stir together to form a roux. Strain the milk, pour on to the roux and whisk until combined. Cook until thickened, stirring all the time to prevent lumps and sticking. You will end up with a rather unappetizing thick and gloopy white sauce – have faith. Add the cheese and mustard, mix thoroughly until combined, scrape into a shallow dish and spread out to cool, pressing down a layer of clingfilm on top to prevent a skin forming. Once cool, chill in the fridge for an hour or two to firm up.

To shape the croquetas, set yourself up a production line with the beaten egg in a bowl and the breadcrumbs on a plate. Take a generous dessertspoonful of the chilled mixture and shape it into a miniature rugby ball. Drop gently into the egg then lift out and roll in the breadcrumbs until coated all over. Transfer to a clean plate. Repeat with the remaining mixture then chill again for at least 30 minutes. They will rest quite happily in the fridge for 24 hours.

To cook, heat a deep-fat fryer to 180°C and fry in batches for 3 minutes until crisp and golden. Drain on kitchen paper. Alternatively, heat a litre of oil in a large saucepan. When a cube of bread dropped in takes 60 seconds to turn a deep golden brown, the oil is hot enough. Cook in small batches. Overcrowding will result in a dramatic drop in temperature.

24th September

Mojito sorbet

DISTINCTLY GROWN-UP

This is the evening of the second supper club. While I wanted it to be a celebration of all that is perfect about autumn eating, I also wanted to hint that summer had only just left us. Not least because I still had a whole raised bed packed full of mint, which in our house we call the 'mojito bed', as a nod to what is possibly the best cocktail in the world. Mojitos to me are the ultimate summer drink, somehow only tasting at their best when sipped outside in the evening sunshine. With that in mind I wanted to capture that essence of pure summer, the mint, lime, sugar and rum, and turn it into a very grown-up sorbet to serve as a sharp pause between main course and pudding. The egg white is used to emulsify the mixture and soften the texture, producing a sorbet that is truly sublime. I served this in little crystal glasses, dipped in egg white and sugar to give a pretty sparkly rim.

Makes enough for 8 scoops

For the syrup:

250g white sugar

250ml water

A large handful of mint leaves (about 30g)

Zest of 5 limes (reserve fruit for juicing below)

For the sorbet:

Juice of 8 limes (approx. 200ml juice)

100ml white rum

Zest of 3 limes

A few sprigs of fresh mint, leaves picked and finely chopped

1 egg white

Begin by making the sugar syrup. Add the sugar, water, mint leaves and lime zest to a small saucepan and bring up to the boil. Boil steadily for 5 minutes, then turn off the heat and leave to cool and infuse. When completely cold, strain into a bowl and discard the mint and lime zest.

For the sorbet, mix the lime juice and rum into the sugar syrup. Add the lime zest and finely chopped mint. Now taste the mixture – it should be sweet, sharp and minty, just like an intense version of a mojito cocktail. Add a little more lime or mint if necessary. Much as it might be tempting, don't add more rum as alcohol doesn't freeze and your sorbet will never set firm if you do.

In a separate bowl, whisk the egg white until stiff, just as if you were making meringues, and then fold this through the sorbet base. Don't worry if it doesn't mix perfectly – keep stirring it as it freezes, eventually the egg white will combine.

Pour the mixture into a large plastic tub, cover with a lid or piece of foil and place in the freezer until set firm. This will take at least 6 hours, depending on the temperature of your freezer and the depth of the mix. Every hour or two give it a good beating with a metal spoon to mix and break down the ice crystals. For a really smooth sorbet, pulse briefly in a food processor halfway through freezing.

It will keep for a week or so in the freezer, tightly covered to preserve the flavour. But I somehow doubt it will last that long.

Plum, amaretto & almond crumble with proper vanilla custard

Who doesn't love a fruit crumble? Possibly the finest autumn pudding ever invented – give me a fruity pud over a chocolate one any day. In honour of tonight's supper club guests, this one is just a tiny bit special, with a splash of amaretto in the plums and little nubs of toasted almonds hiding in the crumble. But the real reason to make this dish was the jug of gloriously thin and creamy home-made custard that we poured, at room temperature, over the piping hot

crumble. A perfect contrast between hot and cool, sweet and sharp, smooth and crunchy – I cannot think of a better way to showcase my wonderful eggs. My preference, absolutely and always, would be for cold custard and hot crumble. It just works for me, in the same way that hot apple pie and cold, cold ice cream work. But it is not for everyone. A straw poll among family, friends and blog-acquaintances revealed that it's a neat fifty-fifty split between hot custard and cold custard lovers. Which side of the fence do you fall on?

Serves 4

For the custard:
200ml milk
100ml double cream
½ vanilla pod, split lengthways
3 egg yolks
55g caster sugar

For the crumble:
200g plain flour
125g cold unsalted butter, cut into small dice
50g whole blanched almonds
75g golden caster sugar

For the plums:
700g plums, stones removed, cut into bite-size pieces
2–3 tbsp amaretto
1–2 tbsp caster sugar

I make the custard first so it has plenty of time to cool to my perfect serving temperature. In a heavy-based saucepan, heat the milk and cream, together with the split vanilla pod, until just below boiling point. Turn off the heat and leave to infuse for 30 minutes, before taking out the vanilla pod and scraping the little black seeds back into the creamy milk, stirring them through.

In a large bowl, whisk together the egg yolks and sugar until thickened. Pour the vanilla milk over and whisk thoroughly. Wash and dry the saucepan, pour in the uncooked custard and cook over the lowest possible heat until it thickens to the consistency of double cream. This will take longer than you might imagine – at least 15 minutes – and you need to watch it like a hawk. If you keep stirring, almost constantly, and do not let it get anywhere near simmering point, you should have no problems. But the custard can separate if it gets too hot too quickly, so keep a large metal bowl near you just in case. If it begins to split, quickly pour the lot into the bowl and whisk as fast as you can to cool it down and, I hope, rescue it from scrambling.

At this point I strained my custard into a jug and covered it in a layer of pressed-down clingfilm to stop a skin forming, setting it to one side to cool to room temperature. If you prefer hot custard, leave it in the pan, also pressed with clingfilm, ready to warm through when the crumble is ready. It is not essential to strain it but I think it's worth it for a super smooth result.

Preheat the oven to 180°C/Gas 4. Lightly butter an ovenproof dish and tip in the prepared plums. Sprinkle over the amaretto and sugar. Set aside.

Make the crumble in a large bowl by rubbing the flour and butter together between finger and thumb until it resembles breadcrumbs. A delicate touch with cool fingers will produce the light, crisp crumble you are after. You can do this in a food processor if you prefer but the result can be heavier and slightly cake-like.

Toast the almonds for a couple of minutes in a dry frying pan until golden brown, then tip on to a chopping board and cut up roughly. Stir the almond pieces through the crumble along with the sugar. Sprinkle the crumbs lightly over the plums, trying not to pat down or level too vigorously or you will lose the valuable air that creates a lovely open texture. Bake for around 40 minutes until the crumble is crisp and golden brown. Serve hot with the custard poured generously over the top.

Caramelized onion, Cheddar & rosemary scone bread

Having spent the morning in the garden clearing the first fall of autumn leaves, I was ravenously hungry. I rustled up this scone bread to jazz up a tin of tomato soup for lunch when I realized we had no bread for the obligatory dunking. This is one of those versatile recipes where you shouldn't feel too constrained by what you have and haven't got. Treat it as a base to use up odds and ends lurking in the fridge. You could change the herbs or the cheese – sage and blue cheese would be lovely – or even add crisply cooked snippets of bacon if you had some. The trick with any sort of scone, sweet or savoury, is to work quickly and lightly, remembering that a heavy hand will produce a heavy scone. And if impressive height is what you're after, simply don't flatten the scone too much.

Like all scones, this one is best served warm from the oven, cut into wedges and smothered with butter.

Makes 1 loaf, enough for 4

75g butter

1 tbsp olive oil

1 large onion, finely sliced

350g self-raising flour, plus extra for dusting

2–3 sprigs of fresh rosemary, leaves roughly chopped

Salt & freshly ground black pepper

150g mature Cheddar, grated

2 large eggs

4 tbsp milk, plus extra for brushing

Melt about a third of the butter with the olive oil and gently fry the onion until soft and lightly caramelized. It is worth taking a little time over this. Too high a heat and the onion will burn before it has time to soften and release its natural sugars, so keep the heat low and allow about 30 minutes.

Dice the remaining 50g butter into 1cm cubes and add with the flour to a food processor. Pulse until it resembles rough breadcrumbs. Add the rosemary, caramelized onions, salt and pepper, and pulse again until mixed. Finally add 120g of the cheese, the eggs and milk and pulse for one more time until the mixture comes together as a rough dough.

Preheat the oven to 180°C/Gas 4. Tip the scone dough on to a lightly floured work surface and gently bring together into a ball. Flatten to a disc of about 2–3 cm high and carefully lift on to a baking tray. Brush the top with a little milk and sprinkle the remaining Cheddar over.

Bake for about 35 minutes or until the top is golden brown and the scone is cooked through.

30th September

Italian pear & ginger baked cheesecake

A MARRIAGE MADE IN HEAVEN

This is a different beast to the more traditional lemon cheesecake I baked in August. For a start, it has no real base to speak of, just a light scattering of gingernut crumbs, and being made with ricotta it has a slightly grainy, more open texture than its cream-cheese counterpart. I was inspired to make it after a visit to my local greengrocer's, a wonderful and rather old-fashioned shop that specializes in seasonal English produce. At this time of year there are shelves overflowing with autumnal fruits, including many unusual heritage varieties of plums, apples and pears.

Serves 6–8 generously

25g butter, melted

50g gingernut biscuits, finely crushed (about 5 biscuits)

750g ricotta cheese

250g mascarpone

250g caster sugar

50g self-raising flour

6 eggs

½ tsp vanilla extract

140g stem ginger in syrup, roughly diced, plus 4 tbsp syrup

3 fat firm pears – comice or blush are lovely – peeled, quartered & cores removed

Icing sugar, to dust (optional)

Preheat the oven to 160°C/Gas 3.

Line the base of a 23–25cm springform tin with baking paper and brush all over with the melted butter. Scatter in the biscuit crumbs and tap around to get a thin but even coating all over the base and sides of the tin. Set aside.

Put the ricotta, mascarpone, sugar and flour in a food processor and blitz until smooth. Alternatively, beat together in a bowl with a wooden spoon, ensuring there are no lumps. Add the eggs, vanilla and chopped stem ginger and process or stir until completely mixed.

Place the pears in a saucepan so they fit in a snug single layer, pour over the ginger syrup and toss to coat. Simmer, covered with a lid or piece of foil, over a low heat for around 10 minutes until soft.

Pour the cheesecake mixture into the prepared tin and level the surface with the flat of a knife. Arrange the poached pears in a fan shape over the surface; don't worry if they sink a little.

Bake in the oven for 1 hour until firm to the touch and a deep golden brown. Remove from the oven and allow to cool in the tin. Once at room temperature, remove from the tin and chill. Serve in wedges, dusted with a little icing sugar if you like.

1st October

Sage tagliatelle with roast pumpkin & Stilton

This began life, like the majority of my cooking, as a dish imagined while I pondered my ingredients, the weather, my mood and the occasion. In this case, the recipe evolved over many months as I watched my pumpkins grow and ripen. I was planning to make tortellini, little stuffed pasta shapes with a filling of Stilton and roasted pumpkin. Indeed, that's what I started making, but as I began working my pasta dough it struck me how dreadfully wasteful it was to cut, roll and shape tortellini. I glanced at the chickens outside and felt bad about wasting their precious eggs, and realized it would simply not be right in this day and age to throw out a third of my dough as I trimmed the pasta shapes. So I stopped and had a rethink. This, then, is the deconstructed version, and utterly delicious it was too, filling and deeply savoury.

Serves 4, generously

For the pasta:

400g '00' pasta flour

4 large eggs

2 tbsp extra virgin olive oil

Sage leaves – a loose handful (about 5g leaves, no stalks), finely chopped

Salt & freshly ground black pepper

For the pumpkin:

1kg pumpkin (or squash), peeled and chopped into 1–2cm cubes

1 large red onion, chopped

3 tbsp olive oil

Salt & freshly ground black pepper

Sage leaves – a loose handful (about 5g leaves, no stalks), roughly chopped

6 cloves garlic, unpeeled

350g Stilton, crumbled

To finish:

60g unsalted butter

Pasta dough can be made by hand, in a food processor or (the way I tend to do it) in a food mixer with a dough hook. By hand, add the flour to a large bowl, break in the eggs and add the remaining ingredients, including a generous seasoning of salt and pepper. Mix together with a wooden spoon until you have a rough dough, then tip on to the work surface and knead for a few minutes until it is smooth and elastic. If using a processor, simply add all the ingredients to a bowl and pulse until you have a rough dough, then tip on to the worktop and knead. In a food mixer, you add all the ingredients and let the dough hook do the mixing and kneading for you. Whichever way you make it, it is important to let the dough rest in the fridge for at least 30 minutes before you roll it; this allows it to relax and become more workable. It will keep, well wrapped, in the fridge for a couple of days if you want to make it in advance.

The easiest way to roll pasta is to use a pasta machine. Cut the dough into quarters and feed each piece through the rollers, reducing the setting on the machine to roll it thinner and thinner. Once you have a thin sheet, cover it loosely with clingfilm and continue with the other pieces. You can also shape your dough into sheets with a rolling pin and a bit of elbow grease. Cut the sheets into tagliatelle, either rustically by hand, or as I did by using the ribbon cutter on my machine. Hang the ribbons over a coat hanger and leave to dry a little while you cook the pumpkin.

Preheat the oven to 180°C/Gas 4. In a large roasting tin, toss the pumpkin (or squash) and red onion in the olive oil and season generously with pepper and less generously with salt. Stir through the sage, tuck in the cloves of garlic, and roast for around 25 minutes until the pumpkin is tender and caramelizing at the edges.

Turn off the oven. Fish out the garlic cloves and set aside. Sprinkle the crumbled Stilton over the roast vegetables and return to the falling heat of the oven so the cheese gently melts while you cook the pasta and make the butter sauce.

Set a large pan of salted water to boil for cooking the pasta.

Once it is vigorously boiling, lower in the tagliatelle and cook until *al dente* – around 3–4 minutes. Drain and return to the pan.

To make the sauce, melt the butter in a small heavy-based frying pan. Allow it to bubble over a medium heat for a couple of minutes until it has turned a nutty golden brown, taking care it doesn't burn. Remove from the heat. Peel the roast garlic and squidge it to a purée with the flat of a knife. Mix it into the butter, pour over the pasta and toss until it is coated all over.

Serve the pasta in wide bowls topped with the pumpkin and melted Stilton and stir through as you eat.

4th October

Bacon, parsnip & cheese brunch muffins

Breakfast at the weekend deserves something a tiny bit more thought out than the usual bowl of cereal or hastily made toast. It feels quietly luxurious to make more of a meal out of it, taking the time to drink a coffee and chat, simply enjoying that I don't need to tell anyone to hurry up. Savoury muffins are something I sometimes make to fill that role. They are quick and easy to knock up and the permutations are numberless. On a whim, today's muffins contain grated parsnip. I had one lurking in the fridge and I thought, if you can have a carrot cake, then surely you can have a parsnip muffin. Celery, gently softened in a little butter or oil, would be good too, as would red onion or grated courgette. Add a few chopped herbs, a bit of bacon, chorizo or shredded ham, and some sort of crumbled hard cheese … experiment to your heart's content, just keep roughly the same ratios of flour to egg and yogurt.

Makes 12

6 rashers smoked streaky bacon, cut into 1cm strips

1 fat parsnip, coarsely grated

150g plain flour

100g wholemeal plain flour

2 tsp baking powder

½ tsp bicarbonate of soda

½ tsp smoked paprika

130g cheese, crumbled or grated (e.g. Cheddar, feta, Manchego)

250g Greek (or other wholemilk) yogurt

2 eggs

4 tbsp olive oil

Salt & freshly ground black pepper

Preheat the oven to 180°C/Gas 4. Line a 12-hole muffin tin with paper cases.

Fry the bacon for a few minutes until crisp but still succulent. Add the parsnip, stir through, turn off the heat and set aside.

In a large bowl, mix together both flours, the baking powder and bicarbonate of soda and the paprika. Stir through the bacon and parsnip, and about 100g of the cheese, ensuring it is well mixed.

In a small bowl, beat together the yogurt, eggs and olive oil, and season with a little salt and pepper. Pour into the large bowl with the dry ingredients and fold to roughly combine. Don't worry about a few lumps and bumps, or even little bits of unmixed flour: muffins, savoury and sweet, benefit greatly from a light touch.

Spoon into the muffin cases, sprinkle over the rest of the cheese and bake for about 20 minutes until deeply golden and springy to the touch.

These are best eaten while fresh and warm, possibly smeared with a little butter. They also freeze really well so you could always make a double batch and freeze half for a later date. To serve, defrost, then warm slightly in the oven to bring them back to life.

7th October

Cauliflower bhajis with raita

FOR A CURRY-FEST

On a miserable wet weekend I love nothing better than spending the afternoon preparing a feast for the evening, to be shared with friends and accompanied by much wine and laughter. One of my favourite themes for such a feast is a curry night, not the opening of an array of take-away boxes, but the slow simmering of numerous dishes, filling the house with a heady and tempting aroma. I am a huge fan of Madhur Jaffrey, and her *Curry Bible* is a real treasure trove of spiced dishes from all over the world. It is one of the most thumbed and food-splattered cookery books in my kitchen, a sure sign of its usefulness. Tonight, before we moved on to curries, dhal and pilau rice, I wanted to make a crunchy, lightly spiced bhaji with cauliflower and onion. It's probably fair to say that authentic bhajis don't contain egg, but I find it helps bind the batter together so the bhajis are less likely to fall apart on frying.

Serves 4–6 as a starter

For the bhajis:

200g chickpea (gram) flour

1 egg

A generous pinch of salt

1 tbsp mustard seeds

1 tbsp cumin seeds

½ tsp turmeric

Approx. 100ml cold water

½ cauliflower, broken up into small florets

1 onion, finely sliced

1–2 green chillies, finely chopped

Vegetable oil for deep-frying

Fresh coriander leaves, to garnish

For the raita:

250ml full-fat yogurt

½ cucumber, grated

Small bunch of mint, leaves picked & finely chopped

1 clove garlic, crushed

Salt & freshly ground black pepper

In a mixing bowl, beat together the flour, egg, salt and spices, adding just enough water to make a really thick paste-like batter. Add the cauliflower, onion and chilli and mix well, ensuring everything is coated all over. The mixture should be sticky but quite dry. Set aside while you prepare the raita.

Mix the yogurt with the cucumber, mint and garlic. Season to taste with salt and pepper.

I cooked my bhajis in a deep-fat fryer with the thermostat set to 180°C. If you don't have one, a big stock pot with a good litre or so of oil will be fine. To test the temperature, drop in a cube of bread – if it turns golden in a minute or so it is hot enough. When cold, the oil can be strained back into the bottle for another time.

Whichever way you fry, drop heaped dessertspoonfuls of battered veg into the hot oil and cook for a couple of minutes, then flip over and cook the other side. Don't overcrowd the pan or the temperature will drop dramatically and they won't crisp up. Drain on kitchen roll and repeat until you have used all the mix.

Serve the bhajis piled on a plate, sprinkled with a little chopped coriander, and with a dish of raita on the side.

9th October

Quick and simple sponge recipe to make two birthday cakes

My children's birthdays are a day apart, one on the 9th and one on the 10th of October, and I still haven't quite worked out if this was bad planning or good luck. It does mean that, at least while they are young and relatively compliant, they can have joint parties. But it also means the few days leading up to their birthdays are a touch hectic, to say the least. Anything I can do to cut down on stress is very welcome. This year they each had their own cake; last year I think I got away with one between two. Little did they know it was basically the same cake just decorated in a different way. This is my failsafe vanilla sponge recipe. I turn to it often and know it by heart, and if I'm pushed it can be on the table, warm and filled with oozing jam, in 30 minutes flat. This time I enhanced the mirage of difference with a few drops of food colouring in the sponge, pink for Eve and green for Izaac. The girly cake was then decorated with pink fondant icing and dotted all over with pink and white baby marshmallows, utterly sickly but delightful to a four-year-old. And the other one had slightly more sophisticated zingy lemon buttercream and grated dark chocolate. I have given my icing recipes but really this cake is all about customizing to fit your occasion.

Makes 1 double-layer sponge, suitable for filling with jam or butter icing

For the sponge:

180g butter, at room temperature

180g caster sugar

3 eggs

180g self-raising flour

1 tsp baking powder

1 tsp vanilla extract

2–3 tbsp milk

For the pink fondant icing (enough for 1 double-layer sponge):

225g fondant icing sugar, sifted

60g unsalted butter, at room temperature

½ tsp vanilla extract

A few drops red food colouring

1–2 tsbp cold water

For the lemon buttercream (enough for 1 double-layer sponge):

225g icing sugar, sifted

100g unsalted butter, at room temperature

Finely grated zest of 1 lemon

2 tsp lemon juice

Preheat the oven to 180°C/Gas 4. Grease 2 sponge tins of about 20cm in diameter.

Cream together the butter and sugar until pale and fluffy. Using a food mixer, an electric whisk or a large mixing bowl with a wooden spoon will achieve the same result with varying degrees of elbow grease and amounts of time. The food mixer gets my vote for speed.

Add the eggs, one at a time, mixing well between each addition. Sift in the flour and baking powder and beat together. Finally add the vanilla extract and enough milk so it combines to a soft batter. Divide the mixture between the two tins and level gently with a spatula. Bake in the oven for about 15–20 minutes or until a skewer inserted in the centre comes out clean. Slide a knife round the edge of each cake and ease out of the tin on to a cooling rack.

For a simple Victoria sponge, allow to cool a little before spreading with jam, sandwiching together and dusting the top with icing sugar. For more elaborate icing allow it to cool completely.

My pink fondant icing was made by simply beating all the ingredients together until it reached a smooth spreadable consistency. The lemon buttercream was made exactly the same way, the water being replaced by a little lemon juice.

15th October

Spanish flan

A CRÈME CARAMEL WITH A HINT OF
ORANGE & CINNAMON

Flan is essentially a type of crème caramel and it is probably Spain's most popular pudding, where they eat it in all manner of flavours, from vanilla to chocolate to coffee. This version is subtly scented with orange and cinnamon. I grew up on 'caramel cream', as we called it, made from a packet with a pint of milk, and it was possibly one of the first things I ever made in the kitchen. There was never enough of the gorgeous sticky caramel sauce but as a bonus I was sometimes allowed to suck on the empty sachet to get access to every last drop. With that in mind, I have made my recipe with plenty of caramel, which I think is the whole point of this simple pudding. This version is far denser and a little more grown up than the packet mixes of my childhood, which I still make for my kids as a real treat from time to time. They, too, fight over who gets to suck on the sauce sachet, just as my brother and I did.

Serves 6

300ml double cream	75g caster sugar
300ml milk	
Finely grated zest of 2 oranges	*For the caramel:*
1 cinnamon stick	200g caster sugar
5 eggs	100ml cold water

Put the cream, milk, orange zest and cinnamon stick in a heavy-based saucepan. Bring slowly up to the boil and simmer gently for a couple of minutes. Turn off the heat and leave to infuse for 2 hours.

To make the caramel, tip the sugar into a saucepan and add the water. Bring up to the boil and simmer steadily for about 15 minutes until the caramel turns a deep golden brown. Don't stir it, just give the pan a little wiggle from side to side every now and then to make sure it is caramelizing evenly. The trick to good caramel is bravery: you need to dare to take it a shade darker while being mindful of not burning it. You can't taste it to see if it's done as the temperature will be thermonuclear, so use your nose as a guide – it should smell pleasingly bitter but not acrid. Once you are happy with it, pour it into a shallow ovenproof dish. A glass pie dish is ideal.

Preheat the oven to 140°C/Gas 2. Whisk the eggs and sugar in a large bowl until well combined but not too aerated. Strain the infused cream over the eggs and sugar and mix gently, again without adding many bubbles – this is a dense creamy pudding rather than a light one. Place the baking dish in a large roasting tin and slowly pour the custard over the caramel. Add enough boiling water to the tin to come halfway up the sides of the dish and carefully transfer to the oven.

Bake the flan in its water bath for 45 minutes to an hour. It is difficult to be precise about the cooking time as it depends on the size and depth of the dish. It is ready when it is just set with still the faintest hint of wobble. Remove from the oven and allow to cool in the water bath, then transfer to the fridge and chill for at least 5 hours.

When you are ready to serve, run a knife around the edge of the dish, lay a large plate over the top and quickly invert the whole lot to release the pudding.

Chakchouka with merguez sausages & baked eggs

Chakchouka is a gorgeous, delicately spiced pepper, tomato and egg stew from Tunisia. Once the vegetables are cooked and the sauce is thick and rich you crack eggs on the surface and there they poach gently to your liking. I was delighted to discover recently that one of my local butcher's shops makes its own merguez, spicy North African lamb sausages, and I decided to add them to my stew for something more substantial. Generous hunks of bread to dip in were all we needed as an accompaniment. This serves two for supper but can easily be doubled, using a larger frying pan.

Serves 2

1 tsp caraway seeds	1 tsp dried chilli flakes
1 tsp cumin seeds	2 cloves garlic, finely sliced
1 tbsp olive oil	1 x 400g tin chopped tomatoes
4–6 merguez sausages (or other spiced sausage)	Salt & freshly ground black pepper
2 red peppers, deseeded & sliced	2 eggs
1 yellow or green pepper, deseeded & sliced	A few sprigs of flat-leaf parsley, leaves roughly chopped, to serve

Toast the caraway and cumin seeds in a dry frying pan for a couple of minutes, taking care not to burn them. As soon as you smell their aroma wafting up from the pan, tip into a mortar and roughly crush with the pestle.

Add the olive oil to the same pan and fry the sausages for a few minutes on each side until golden. Remove to a plate, cut each in half and set aside.

Now add the peppers to the same pan and fry over a medium-high heat for 10 minutes or so until they are soft and just starting to catch a little at the edges. Add the crushed seeds, chilli flakes and sliced garlic and fry for another 30 seconds. Then pour in the tomatoes, add the sausage pieces and bring up to a simmer. Turn the heat down and allow to cook and thicken for around 15–20 minutes, by which time the sauce should be rich and have an almost jam-like consistency. Taste and season with a little salt and pepper.

Using the back of a wooden spoon, make 2 hollows in the surface of the stew. Break an egg into each hollow and sprinkle over a little salt and pepper. Continue to simmer over a fairly low heat until the eggs are cooked to your liking – around 10 minutes for just-set white and a runny yolk. Scatter with the parsley and serve immediately.

21st October

Warm brioche for breakfast

PERFECT FOR BREAKFAST

This was a bit of an experiment. I had never made a brioche loaf before. Plus this slightly sweet, rich bread is not my ideal breakfast; I prefer something more savoury in the mornings. But my kids love it and it uses plenty of eggs so I thought I should give it a go. It needs to be started the day before you want to eat it, and I have to concede it was worth the effort. Served warm with lashings of apricot jam, it really was a delicious treat. This recipe is best made in a food mixer with a dough hook as there is a lot of kneading involved.

Serves 4 plentifully

75ml milk

2 tsp dried yeast

25g caster sugar

375g strong white bread flour, plus extra for dusting

½ tsp salt

4 eggs, plus 1 extra for glazing

200g unsalted butter in cubes, softened to room temperature, plus extra for greasing

Grease a 25cm loose-based springform tin and lightly dust with flour.

Warm the milk to 'blood temperature': that is, if you were to stick your finger in it, it would feel neither hot nor cold but pretty much the same temperature as you. I find the easiest way to do this is to give it 20 seconds on high in the microwave, but warm it in a small pan if you prefer. Sprinkle over the yeast and sugar and mix well. Set aside for 10 minutes – it should develop a foamy head.

Put the flour, salt and eggs into the bowl of a food mixer. With the dough hook, mix and knead for 5 minutes on a low setting, about a third of full power – my mixer was set to level 3. If you were to do this by hand it would take a good 10 minutes.

Add the butter a few bits at a time, kneading well between each addition. Again, you can do this by hand but it is far easier in a mixer. Once all the butter is in, continue to mix for another 7–8 minutes. The dough should be shiny and stretchy. Tip on to a lightly floured worktop and cut into 8 even-sized pieces. Roll each piece into a ball. Put one ball in the centre of the tin, and arrange the other 7 around the outside, like a flower. Now cover the tin tightly with a double layer of clingfilm and refrigerate overnight.

The following morning, remove the brioche from the fridge, take off the clingfilm and allow to rise at room temperature for an hour.

Gently brush the surface of the brioche with the beaten egg. Cook in a preheated oven set at 180°C/Gas 4 for about 35 minutes until deep golden brown on the surface. Release from the springform tin and allow to cool just a little before serving still warm.

25th October

Carrot & cumin tart

This midweek tart was very cheap but exceedingly cheerful, not least because of its gorgeous sunny colour. It's equally good hot or cold, making it useful for packed lunches too. I first ate something similar during my frugal student days – I have a vague memory of one of my friends presenting it to me for supper and being pleasantly surprised that what is basically a carrot quiche could be so delicious. Even these days when money is not so tight I still find it useful to have a few very economical dishes in my repertoire. It feels good to eat humbly from time to time, and for the sake of the planet I think we could all do with eating a little less meat. You could, of course, make it more indulgent by replacing some of the milk with a little cream if you happened to have some. Don't be alarmed at the volume of carrots; they will cook right down. We ate this with a simple side dish of frozen peas which I had sautéed gently in butter with a handful of chopped spring onions and a little mint.

Serves 4

For the pastry:

200g plain flour, plus extra for dusting

100g butter

A pinch of salt, a generous grind of pepper

3 tbsp cold water

For the filling:

3 tsp cumin seeds

2 tbsp olive oil

2 cloves garlic, crushed

½ tsp smoked paprika

1kg carrots, peeled & grated

1 tsp vegetable bouillon powder, or ½ vegetable stock cube, crumbled

200ml milk (or a mix of milk and cream)

3 eggs, plus one extra yolk

Salt & freshly ground black pepper

30g Parmesan or other hard cheese, grated

In a food processor, pulse together the flour and butter until it just resembles fine breadcrumbs. Add the salt and pepper and pulse again to mix. Add the cold water and pulse again until it just starts to come together in a rough ball. Don't over-process or the pastry can become tough. Tip on to a sheet of clingfilm and gently press into a ball. Wrap tightly and chill for 30 minutes in the fridge.

While the pastry is resting, prepare the filling. In a large deep frying pan, dry-fry the cumin seeds for a minute or two. As soon as you smell their aroma wafting up from the pan, add the olive oil, garlic and paprika. Fry gently for a minute, then add the carrots and the bouillon powder or stock cube and a splash, just a couple of tablespoons or so, of cold water. Cook gently for 10 minutes until the carrots have softened down, then remove from the heat and allow to cool a little.

Mix the milk, eggs and extra egg yolk in a jug and season generously.

When you are ready to make the pastry case, preheat the oven to 200°C/Gas 6, placing a heavy baking tray on the shelf to get hot.

Lightly dust the worktop with a little flour and roll out the pastry to fit a loose-based metal flan tin of about 25cm diameter. If it starts to crack a little at the edges, gently pinch it back together to keep the shape as round as possible. Lay the pastry over the tin, and gently lift and press it down into the bottom. Roll the rolling pin over the top, cutting the excess pastry off. Line with baking paper and fill with baking beans. Slide on to the hot baking tray and cook for 15 minutes. Remove from the oven, take out the paper and beans and return to the oven for a further 5 minutes to dry out.

Reduce oven temperature to 180°C/Gas 4. Spread the cooked carrot over the pastry case and gently pour the egg and milk mixture over. Finally sprinkle with the cheese and return to the oven to cook for about 25 minutes until set.

31st October
Coconut marshmallows

FOR HALLOWEEN TOASTING

I found myself promising the kids I'd make them home-made marshmallows for toasting on Halloween, but to be honest I find the plain ones a little dull. The ones I like are mixed with fresh fruit or alcohol and covered in cocnut, but these would be no use for

toasting, burning long before the marshmallow had started to ooze properly. So the experiment was to add coconut into the mixture so that the flavour and texture were integral to the sweet rather than just on the surface. It worked rather well and made them much more interesting. The little darlings protested at my tinkering but in the end they conceded that it was *quite* a good idea. Praise indeed. Note that marshmallows will keep for several days so can be made ahead of the bonfire.

Cuts into about 36 marshmallows

2 tbsp icing sugar mixed with 2 tbsp cornflour, for coating

2 egg whites

500g granulated sugar

250ml cold water

8 sheets of leaf gelatine (16g), soaked in cold water for 10 minutes to soften

100g desiccated coconut

Prepare a 20cm square baking tin by spraying lightly all over with non-stick cooking spray or brushing with a little vegetable oil. Add a little of the icing sugar and cornflour mix and tap around the tin so it is evenly coated. Save the rest for the marshmallow cubes. Set the tin aside.

Put the egg whites in the bowl of a food mixer and whisk until they hold stiff peaks. Turn off the mixer while you make the hot sugar syrup.

Put the sugar and water in a pan and warm over a low heat until the sugar is completely dissolved, then bring up to the boil and allow to cook over a high heat until it reaches what is known as the 'firm ball' stage. An easy way to test for this is to drop a teaspoon of syrup into a glass of cold water. It should form a firm 'toffee-ish' ball that holds its shape. If you have a sugar thermometer, it will read 122°C.

With the mixer set on low, start to beat the egg whites once more. Add the hot syrup in a steady trickle, mixing continuously. The mixture will turn creamy and look like a stiff shiny meringue. Remove the leaves of gelatine from the cold water and squeeze out any excess, then add them to the mixer and whisk again until completely combined. Finally add the coconut and mix again. The mixture should be thick, shiny and just about pourable. Scrape into the prepared tin and level quickly with the flat of a table knife. Leave to set in a cool place, but not in the fridge, for 4–6 hours (or overnight).

When the marshmallow has set, sprinkle a little more of the icing sugar and cornflour on to the surface of a chopping board. Turn the marshmallow out on to the board and cut into squares. Toss the squares in the rest of the icing sugar and cornflour until they are evenly coated all over. Thread on to skewers or toasting forks and toast for a few minutes over the embers of your bonfire.

2nd November

Baked eggs with wild mushrooms & cream

I adore mushrooms, particularly wild ones with their intense, earthy, woodland aroma. I have always promised myself I'll take a course in gathering wild mushrooms to learn which are both good and safe to eat. In the meantime I have to be content with buying them as and when they appear in the shops. They are pretty pricey, so I cooked this dish with some cultivated chestnut mushrooms from the supermarket, plus a handful of wild girolles and pieds de mouton I found in a lovely local deli. Rich with sherry, cream and garlic, this is a real treat of a dish to share with your loved one on a chilly autumn evening. Serve with plenty of bread to dip into it. A glass of cold dry sherry alongside would be a fitting accompaniment – it worked for me!

Serves 2 for lunch or a light supper

30g unsalted butter

2 generous handfuls of mushrooms, a mixture of wild & cultivated, torn into bite-size pieces

A couple of sprigs of thyme, leaves picked

1 clove garlic, finely sliced

2 tbsp dry sherry – I like dry oloroso for its rich nutty flavour

200ml double cream

Salt & freshly ground black pepper

2 eggs

A little flat-leaf parsley, roughly chopped, to garnish

Preheat the oven to 180°C/Gas 4.

Melt the butter in a small frying pan over a low heat and add the mushrooms and thyme. Sweat very gently for around 10 minutes until the mushrooms are soft, tender and aromatic.

Add the garlic and fry for a further minute or two before pouring in the sherry. Increase the heat and let it evaporate for a couple of minutes. Pour in the cream and season with salt and black pepper. Simmer for a further 1–2 minutes to allow the sauce to thicken, then divide between 2 small baking dishes.

Use the back of a spoon to make a hollow in the centre of each dish and crack an egg into it. Season the top of the egg with a touch more salt and pepper. Bake in the oven for 12–15 minutes until the white has set and the yolk is cooked to your liking.

Serve straight out of the oven, sprinkled with the flat-leaf parsley, while the dishes are still bubbling.

5th November

Toffee-apple doughnuts for bonfire night, plus a few jam ones for fusspots

Toffee apples were a childhood tradition for me. We made them most years and to me they were the best thing about bonfire night – I loved the look of fireworks but was frightened of the noise. I still have the pale shadow of a decades-old scar on my index finger from a dollop of molten toffee, perhaps the first of many 'cook's injuries' my poor hands would have to endure over the years. Anyhow, in my wisdom this bonfire night I decided I'd like to try a toffee-apple-flavoured doughnut. I cannot get my kids to eat cooked apple for love nor money, so there had to be a few traditional jam-filled ones too. I figure if I keep showing them cooked apple treats, eventually they might be brave enough to try some.

I have to admit I was worried about the chickens during bonfire night which, here in the city, can be reminiscent of Beirut. But I am pleased to say that after much nervous checking from me, the chickens slept soundly on their perches as usual – unlike the dog, who cowered under our bed all night.

Makes 12 doughnuts

For the doughnuts:

1 tsp dried yeast

50ml hand-hot water (use half boiling & half cold)

50g granulated sugar

450g strong white (bread) flour, plus extra for dusting

A pinch of salt

1 egg

150ml lukewarm milk

35g butter, melted & cooled, plus extra butter for greasing the bowl

Vegetable oil for deep-frying

For the toffee icing:

50g butter

3 tbsp milk

110g soft brown sugar

110g icing sugar

1 tsp vanilla extract

For the apple filling:

2 cooking apples, peeled, cored & finely chopped

2–3 tbsp sugar, to taste

For the jam version:

Raspberry or strawberry jam, allow a generous teaspoon per doughnut

Caster sugar for rolling

In a small bowl, mix the dried yeast into the warm water with 1 teaspoon of the sugar, and leave to stand for a few minutes until it starts to form a foam on the surface.

The easiest way to make the dough is in a food mixer with a dough hook. Failing that, a bowl and a wooden spoon, followed by a bit of vigorous kneading, is just as good, if a little more energetic. Either in a mixer or a large bowl, put the flour, the rest of the sugar, salt, egg, milk and melted butter. Finally add the foamy yeast paste. In a mixer, mix with the dough hook and knead for 5 minutes until smooth and elastic. If you are doing it by hand, use a wooden spoon to bring the dough together, then turn on to a lightly floured board and knead for 10 minutes.

Scrape the dough into a large, lightly greased bowl and cover with clingfilm. Leave to rise in a warm place for an hour until it has doubled in size. If you prod it gently and the indentation stays in place, then you know it's ready.

While the dough is rising, prepare both the filling and icing. For the icing, melt the butter in a heavy-based saucepan, and add about half the milk and the brown sugar. Bring up to the boil and cook for 1 minute, stirring to ensure the sugar has dissolved. Take the pan off the heat and allow to cool for 5 minutes, then beat in the remaining milk, icing sugar and vanilla extract. You should end up with a rich glossy spreadable icing. Set aside.

To make the apple filling, stew the chopped apple with a mere

splash of water until soft and collapsing. Sweeten to taste with a little sugar, bearing in mind that the icing is really sweet – I like to have quite sharp fruit as a contrast. Allow to cool.

Back to the dough. Turn it on to a floured board and cut into 12 evenly sized pieces. Gently roll each piece into a ball and set aside on a floured baking tray. Cover loosely with a clean tea towel and leave to rise until doubled in size again.

Heat the oil in a deep-fat fryer to 175°C. Alternatively, fill a large stock pot no more than half full with oil and heat until a cube of bread dropped in turns a deep golden brown in a minute. Fry the doughnuts in batches of 2–3 at a time, turning them over with a slotted spoon as they bob to the surface. Lift and drain on kitchen paper and allow to cool until you can handle them.

Scrape the apple purée into a piping bag, insert the nozzle into the middle of each doughnut and squeeze in as much apple as you can without it exploding – a couple of teaspoons is about right. You will end up with a bit of extra apple; I kept mine to eat with some yogurt for breakfast. Spoon the icing over each doughnut and put aside (out of reach!) to allow it to set a little.

If you are filling some with jam, use a piping bag to squeeze the jam into the centre, then roll each doughnut in a dish of sugar.

6th November

Boiled eggs on an impromptu autumn picnic

We awoke to one of those near-perfect autumn days, a milky warm sun burning gently through the morning mist and the trees outside the bedroom window such vivid hues of red, orange and yellow they looked like they were on fire. Quite simply one of those days when it would be wrong to stay inside. So up we rushed. The kids were bundled into warm clothes, a pan of eggs was set to hard-boil, a quick coffee was slurped down, honey sandwiches were made and eaten in seconds. And last but not least, a shoulder of pork hastily shoved into a low oven to slow-roast all day. Off to the Cotswolds we went.

I think hard-boiled eggs are perhaps *the* perfect picnic food. Wrapped safely in their own shell, no need for foil or clingfilm, they are so easily transportable and convenient. So the picnic was boiled eggs, dunked in a little plastic tub of generously seasoned mayo, followed by a packet of pickled onion Monster Munch and a couple of Murray Mints. I am convinced it all tasted so much better for being eaten standing up in the sun-dappled woods.

Both dogs and kids were almost delirious charging about, in the stream, out of the stream, in the mud, out of the mud, climbing trees and collecting fistfuls of crunchy leaves to make Granny a birthday collage. Several hours later we arrived home, filthy and tired, to a house filled with the smell of roast pork. The happiness that comes from simple things is truly wonderful.

12th November

Quince, Marsala and lemon trifle

A LATE-AUTUMN FRUIT PUDDING

I regret that I have come rather late to the fragrant, floral sweetness of quinces. Until this year I had only eaten them as membrillo, the Spanish quince paste that is so delicious with hard cheese. Quinces are not easy to come across – you certainly won't find them at a supermarket – but if you see some in a greengrocer's or Turkish deli, do get them and try this sublime way to eat them. Slow and gentle poaching renders them a gorgeous pink with a sweet, almost fudgy texture. So happy am I to have discovered their charms that I have ordered a tree of my own, a small variety called Lescovacz that comes originally from Serbia. So, fingers crossed, next year I may be making this again with home-grown fruit.

A proper trifle, by which I mean layers of boozy sponge, succulent fruit and puddles of custard all topped with a cloud of softly whipped cream, is my idea of pudding heaven. Absolutely no jelly in any shape or form. Like all trifles, this one benefits from being made the day before you want to eat it. Somehow the flavours and layers need time to settle. This goes some way towards explaining how trifle for breakfast is among my most guilty pleasures.

Serves 4, with leftovers

1 lemon

350ml Marsala

6 tbsp clear honey

400ml cold water

2–3 quinces (about 800g)

300ml whipping cream

For the custard:

300ml milk

150ml double cream

3 large egg yolks

55g caster sugar

1 tsp cornflour

For the sponge:

2 eggs

50g caster sugar

50g plain flour

½ tsp vanilla extract

½ tsp baking powder

Finely grate the zest from the lemon and reserve for the custard. Squeeze the juice into a large saucepan. Add about half the Marsala, the honey and water. Bring up to the boil and stir until the honey has dissolved. Reduce the heat to a very low simmer.

Using a sharp knife with much care – quinces are exceptionally hard – cut the fruit into quarters and chop out the core. Peel each piece and drop straight into the syrup; the flesh will discolour quickly if left out in the air. If the quinces are rather large, cut each quarter in half again. Cover the pan snugly (a piece of foil well tucked over the edge will do if you don't have a lid) and simmer the fruit until very tender. This will take about an hour. You might need to add a splash more water if it looks dry. During cooking the flesh will deepen in colour to a pinky tinge. When the quince is done, set it aside to cool in its syrup.

While the fruit is cooking, make the custard by warming the milk and cream together in a heavy-based saucepan. In a large bowl whisk together the egg yolks, sugar and cornflour with the reserved lemon zest. Pour the creamy milk over the egg yolk mixture and whisk together thoroughly. Wash and dry the saucepan, pour in the uncooked custard and cook over the lowest possible heat until it thickens to the consistency of double cream. Keep stirring and mixing as it cooks to make sure there are no hot spots. Set aside to cool, a layer of clingfilm pressed down on the surface to prevent a skin forming.

Next, make the sponge. Preheat the oven to 180°C/Gas 4. Grease and line a large (2lb) loaf tin. Separate the eggs, putting the whites into one mixing bowl and the yolks into another. Add the sugar to the egg yolks and, ideally using an electric whisk, beat for about 5 minutes until the mixture is pale, thick and creamy. Then, with a clean whisk, beat the egg whites until they are stiff. Take a large spoonful of egg white and fold into the yolk and sugar. Sift over half the flour, then fold it in gently. Add the vanilla extract and whisk until combined. Add the rest of the egg white and fold, followed by the rest of the flour and the baking powder. Pour into the loaf tin and bake for 20–25 minutes until springy and slightly shrinking away from the edge of the tin. Remove from the oven and allow to cool before cutting into slices 1cm thick, discarding the end pieces.

Once the quinces, custard and sponge are all cool, you can begin assembling the trifle. Take a large bowl – glass is best, so you can see the layers – and put a layer of cake slices in the bottom, trying to limit the gaps between the sponge if possible.

You may not need to use it all. Pour over the remaining Marsala, allowing it to soak into the sponge, then add the pieces of quince. Add enough of the syrup so the fruit is just about covered but not swimming. Pour over the custard. Finally, whip the cream until it forms soft peaks and spread lightly over the top. I like to leave my trifle pure and unadorned but you could garnish with a little extra lemon zest if you liked.

Refrigerate for at least 6 hours before serving.

19th November

Two unconventional moussakas

Unconventional and inauthentic these moussakas may be, but they are also delicious and a great option for feeding a crowd. Made for a weekend lunch for carnivores and vegetarians, one was prepared with beef (lamb mince not being a favourite of mine), and the other with slices of pumpkin from the garden, roasted with rosemary and garlic then mixed with tasty green lentils. The recipes are easily doubled up, and can be frozen assembled and uncooked. If you are cooking from cold, add another 15 minutes or so to the baking time.

When I did home economics at school, 'browning' the meat was a term frequently bandied about that seemed to translate as sweating mince until it was a watery grey. Now I am more confident in the kitchen I can declare with absolute certainty that this is not what it means. When a recipe calls for browning, cook over as high a heat as possible. You are looking for caramelization to maximize and intensify flavour. Another cooking 'rule' we are often told is that it is essential to salt and sweat aubergines after we cut them. This used to help extract any bitterness from the flesh. But thankfully, this step is completely unnecessary for the modern strains of aubergine.

Beef & aubergine moussaka

Serves 4 generously

500g quality minced beef (use lamb if you prefer)

4 tbsp olive oil

1 large onion, chopped

3 cloves garlic, finely chopped

250ml white wine

1 x 400g tin chopped tomatoes

1 tbsp tomato purée

2 bay leaves

1 tsp dried thyme

1 tsp dried oregano

1 tsp ground cinnamon

1 tsp ground allspice

A pinch of sugar

200ml water

Salt & freshly ground pepper

2 large aubergines, cut across into 1cm slices

For the cheese topping:

500ml milk

1 bay leaf, fresh or dried

¼ whole nutmeg, grated

50g butter

50g plain flour

25g Parmesan, grated

Salt & freshly ground pepper

2 eggs, lightly beaten

25g mature Cheddar, or extra Parmesan, grated

Preheat the oven to 200°c/ Gas 6.

In a large frying pan, brown the mince in half the olive oil over a high heat. Resist the temptation to stir too much or you will reduce the temperature in the pan and the meat will sweat. When it starts to colour and catch a little, turn it over and around in the pan and let it colour some more. Stir through the onion, reduce the heat to medium and fry for a further 10 minutes. Add the garlic, stir briefly to mix, then pour in the wine and let it simmer for a couple more minutes. Stir through the tomatoes and tomato purée, all the herbs and spices and the sugar. Finally pour in the water, season with a little salt and pepper and bring up to the boil. Reduce the heat to a very gentle simmer and cook for around an hour. This long, slow cooking will intensify the flavour and soften the mince beautifully, so try not to rush it. Once cooked, taste to check the seasoning, adding a little more salt and pepper if necessary.

While the mince is cooking, lay the aubergines in a single layer on a roasting tin. Brush with the remaining olive oil and roast in the oven for about 30 minutes until they are soft and golden brown at the edges.

Make the topping by bringing the milk up to the boil with the bay leaf and nutmeg, then simmering gently for 10 minutes to give it time to infuse. In a separate pan, melt the butter. Stir in the flour to form a thick paste, a roux, and cook gently for a minute. Pour over the milk, bay leaf and all, whisking as you pour to prevent any lumps forming. Bring the sauce up to the boil and cook, stirring all the time, until it has thickened. Turn off the heat and stir through the Parmesan. Season to taste with a little salt and pepper. Allow to cool for a few minutes before stirring the eggs in.

Assemble the moussaka in a deep rectangular or square ovenproof dish. Start with about half the mince in the base of the dish, then top with half the aubergine. Add the remaining mince, followed by the rest of the aubergine. Finally pour over the cheese sauce and sprinkle with the Cheddar. Bake for 25–30 minutes until golden brown and bubbling.

Pumpkin & green lentil moussaka

This moussaka uses the same cheese topping as in the version above but with a rich vegetarian filling of garlicky roasted pumpkin and plump green lentils. I used a pumpkin from the garden but a butternut squash would be great too. And if you don't have green lentils then these could be substituted with brown or Puy lentils. Smoked paprika, readily available in supermarkets, is a really useful spice, adding an intensely savoury depth of flavour that can sometimes be lacking in vegetarian cooking.

Serves 4 generously

900g pumpkin or squash, peeled & sliced 1cm thick

3 tbsp olive oil

1 tsp hot smoked paprika

2 heads of garlic, whole & unpeeled

2–3 sprigs of rosemary

Salt & freshly ground black pepper

200g green lentils

1 onion, finely chopped

750ml vegetable stock

2 bay leaves

For the cheese topping:
See Beef and aubergine recipe on page 202

Preheat the oven to 200°c/ Gas 6.

Put the pumpkin slices into a large roasting tin and drizzle over the olive oil. Sprinkle over the smoked paprika and tuck in the garlic bulbs and rosemary sprigs. Season with a little salt and black pepper. Roast in the oven for 20–30 minutes or so, until the pumpkin is lightly caramelized at the edges and soft when pierced with the tip of a knife. Remove from the oven. Take out the garlic and let it cool for a few minutes before squeezing the cloves out of the skin back into the roasting pan.

Meanwhile, add the lentils and onion to a pan and pour over the stock. Add the bay leaves and a little black pepper but no salt as it would toughen the lentil skins. Bring up to the boil and reduce the heat to a steady simmer. Cook, uncovered, for around 20 minutes until the lentils are just tender but still with a little bite. Pour the lentils and the remaining cooking liquid into the roasting tin with the cooked pumpkin. Stir gently to mix, taking care not to break up the pumpkin too much. Tip the whole lot into a deep baking dish.

Make the topping as in the recipe above, and pour it over the lentils and pumpkin. Sprinkle the Cheddar over the top. Bake for 25–30 minutes until golden brown and bubbling.

Korean egg toast: an Asian egg sarnie with carrot & cabbage

I admit that when I read about 'egg toast', a hugely popular Korean street food dish, I was more than a little sceptical. I love an egg sarnie as much as the next person, but the most simple description of this is as a carrot and cabbage omelette dusted with brown sugar and dripping with ketchup. Unconvinced? Please bear with me on this one! Luckily for me, one of the mums I see daily on the school run comes from Korea, and she vouched for both its popularity and its deliciousness, so I knew I had to give it a whirl. Apparently the real deal is made with the cheapest, whitest, thinnest sliced loaf you can find. Not having any of that to hand I made do with wholemeal, sliced thinly, and it tasted pretty darn good.

Serves 1

2 eggs
½ carrot, grated
Loose handful of cabbage, finely chopped
Salt & freshly ground black pepper
25g unsalted butter
2 slices bread

To serve:
Brown sugar, a little pinch
Tomato ketchup, to taste
Chilli sauce, to taste

Whisk the eggs in a small bowl, then add the carrot and cabbage and mix well. Season with a little salt and black pepper. Set aside.

Melt the butter in a small, preferably non-stick, frying pan. When it is foaming, add the slices of bread and, pressing down with a spatula, fry them until crisp. Turn over and fry on the other side. Remove to a plate and keep warm.

Pour the egg mixture into the pan and allow it to spread evenly. Cook for a couple of minutes, drawing the sides in and stirring a little, just like making an omelette.

When the egg is just set, fold it in half and lay it on one of the pieces of fried bread. Sprinkle over a little brown sugar, followed by a squirt of ketchup. I also added a few drops of fiery chilli sauce as I felt like a bit of a kick.

Top with the other slice of bread and eat immediately – ideally, standing up!

28th November

Far Breton with Armagnac prunes

My happiest memories seem to involve either eating food or the aroma of food being prepared. Call it a passion for cooking, or plain and simple greed, it is just the way I am. Just as with the *pastéis de Belém* on page 13, a version of this tart was eaten on a long ago holiday, this time a trip to Paris as a teenager. More years have passed than I care to count, but I can still remember how I felt as I bit into it, a thick dense wedge of baked custard, studded with fat, succulent, boozy prunes. If I concentrate hard enough I swear I can taste it now. I had no idea then what I was eating, just that it was a wonderful, sublime thing. When I started my great chicken and egg adventure, recreating a version of this tart was one of the first things I knew I must do. After a little research I discovered that what I had eaten was a traditional baked egg and prune tart called *far Breton*, hailing from Brittany in northern France. Here is my recipe, and I am pleased to report it was just as good as I remembered it. It will now become a staple in my cake repertoire, a really useful, delicious cake that keeps well for days and is just perfect with a cup of coffee.

Makes 1 cake, cuttable into 9 generous squares

100ml Armagnac (or amaretto)

300g ready-to-eat prunes

250g plain flour

100g caster sugar

50g melted butter, plus a little
extra for greasing the dish

500ml milk

5 eggs

1 tsp vanilla extract

Icing sugar, to dust

Warm the Armagnac in a small pan, or in the microwave, being careful not to boil it, then pour over the prunes and leave to soak for an hour or two; more time – even overnight – would be good if you had it.

In a large roomy bowl, whisk together the flour, sugar, butter, milk, eggs and vanilla until you have a smooth and glossy batter. Set it aside to rest for at least 30 minutes.

Preheat the oven to 180°C/Gas 4.

Prepare a baking tin, approximately 24cm square, by brushing with a little melted butter, then lining the base and sides with baking paper. You can also bake this in an ovenproof dish, which is the more traditional way, but I like to release it fully from the tin to serve it in thick squares.

Spread the soaked prunes in an even layer over the base of the tin or dish, then pour over the batter. Lift the tin on to a baking tray and carefully transfer to the oven. Cook for 45–55 minutes, or until a skewer inserted into the centre comes out clean.

Allow to cool before turning out from the tin. I like to eat this cold, cut into squares, the surface dusted prettily with a little icing sugar.

30th November
Smoked haddock chowder with poached eggs

Poaching eggs the proper way – that is, freeform in a pan of gently simmering water rather than in a poaching cup – is something I used to be a little nervous of. But now I have so many eggs I have felt more confident about practising. And it's not as tricky as I once thought, provided you follow a few simple rules: use the freshest eggs you can lay your hands on, don't have the water bubbling too fiercely (a gentle simmer is best), and crack the eggs as low to the pan as possible so they don't spread out on hitting the water.

Enough for 4

750ml milk

750g undyed smoked haddock fillet

½ tsp black peppercorns, crushed

2 bay leaves

50g unsalted butter

150g smoked bacon, finely diced

3 sticks celery, finely chopped

2 leeks, washed thoroughly & sliced

2 carrots, peeled & chopped

1 clove garlic, crushed

175ml white wine

2 tsp plain flour

4 medium floury potatoes, peeled & cut into 2cm dice

1 small tin sweetcorn, drained

Generous handful flat-leaf parsley, roughly chopped

Squeeze of lemon juice

For the poached eggs:

1 tsp white wine vinegar

Large fresh eggs, allow 1 per person

Pour the milk into a wide pan and add the fish – you may need to cut it up so it fits in a single layer. Sprinkle over the pepper and tuck in the bay leaves. Bring up to a gentle simmer, cover with a lid or snug-fitting piece of foil, and poach the fish gently for 5–8 minutes. It is done when it flakes easily. Carefully lift the fish from the pan on to a plate and reserve the poaching liquor.

Melt the butter gently in a large, heavy-based saucepan and add the bacon, celery, leeks, carrots and garlic, and sweat over a low heat for around 10 minutes. You want the celery and leeks to be translucent and soft but not coloured at all. Pour over the white wine and allow to bubble and reduce by half. Stir in the flour and add the poaching milk along with its bay leaves and pepper. Stir thoroughly and bring up to the boil. Turn down the heat and add the potatoes and sweetcorn, cover with a lid and simmer gently until the potatoes are cooked through but not falling apart. This will take around half an hour.

While the chowder is simmering, flake the fish, discarding the skin and taking care to remove any small bones. Add the fish to the pan just as the potatoes are cooked – it only needs warming through. Add the parsley and a squeeze of lemon juice to taste. You may also need to add a little salt, depending on how salty the smoked haddock is.

When you are ready to serve, start to poach the eggs by filling a wide-based pan with cold water. Bring up to a rolling boil, add the vinegar and turn the heat down to a gentle simmer. Carefully crack in the eggs, one at a time, and allow to poach undisturbed until they are cooked to your liking. For a yolk that is not too runny, not too dry, this is about 4 minutes. For a runnier yolk, it's about 3 minutes.

Serve the chowder in deep bowls, topped with a poached egg.

Winter

Cold comforts

Winter for me is all about friends. Long Sunday lunches with plenty of warming red wine, a fire blazing in the hearth – basically staying indoors and surrounding myself with my nearest and dearest. But since we've had the chickens I've needed to go outside at least twice a day, every day, and this brings me unexpected joy. I am noticing things about my garden I never have before. Like the way the bare branches of the old lichen-covered apple tree catch the low winter sun. Or how wonderfully scented the tiny bright pink flowers are on a shrub at the top of the garden – some plants even seem to look their best at this time of year, like the tight fountains of the cavolo nero.

But I do still prefer to be indoors, and the kitchen becomes a retreat. The chickens see some benefit to my busy domesticity. All the peelings, from potatoes, carrots, celeriac, parsnips and apples, get cooked down to soft sweet mash that I feed them in the late afternoon. Before I got the chickens, I had heard that egg production can slow or even stop during the winter months. But my girls are laying just as much as ever, with 3 or 4 eggs appearing daily in their nest box. I must be doing something right.

I have often thought how fortunate it is that in the gloomy depths of winter, citrus season is at its peak, just when we need sunshine-bright flavours the most. Oranges, lemons and limes are always in my kitchen at this time of year; I use them in my cooking most days.

Towards the very end of winter I get an itch for spring that is hard to scratch. At this time of year I can often be found nosing through gardening books or ordering plants and seeds online.

Winter is full of recipes to warm the body and nourish the soul.

December

Later-than-planned Christmas pudding
Crème brûlée
Yorkshire pudding with spring greens,
sausages & caramelized shallot gravy
Date, orange & pistachio bread & butter
pudding
Spiced nut meringues with Marsala cream
Festive rabbit & prune pâté
Scrambled egg with smoked salmon
Christmas ham, egg & salsa verde
sandwich
Three ices for New Year's Eve

January

Simple citrus drizzle cake
Eve's pudding
Kedgeree with poached eggs
Coffee custard & bananas
Cheese gougères with creamed leeks
& cider-braised gammon
Chocolate & walnut torte
Nasi goreng with nam prik sauce
Baghdad eggs with herb yogurt
& pitta crisps
Seville orange mousse with almond thins

February

Sublime onion tart
Lime meringue pie
Malaysian egg & aubergine curry with
yellow spiced rice
Rhubarb & almond streusel cake
Pumpkin & pine nut sformato
Marmalade Bakewells
Pancake Day
Warm butterbean, beetroot & egg
winter salad
Lemon curd

1st December

Later-than-planned Christmas pudding

'Stir-up Sunday', the last Sunday in November before the start of advent, is the day when it's traditional to make your Christmas pudding so it matures before the feast. When I was young, Mum made at least one if not two puddings, always following Delia Smith's delicious recipe, and us kids were eagerly on hand to stir through the silver coins, make a wish and hold the string tight while the knot was tied. One memorable Christmas the dog knocked the pudding off the kitchen worktop on Christmas Eve, breaking the bowl in half, then devouring the contents, money and all.

This year I decided to break free of family tradition and devise my own pudding recipe, stuffed full of figs, prunes and dried apple. I have to admit to a few pangs of guilt as I deviated from trusty Delia, but it did feel like I'd finally grown up ... even though I was a few days later making my pud than I should have been.

Makes a 2-pint pudding

130g raisins

130g sultanas

100g dried prunes, chopped

100g dried figs, chopped

100g dried apple, chopped

100g chopped mixed peel

150ml dark rum (or brandy)

120g molasses sugar (or dark muscovado)

120g vegetable or beef suet

70g plain white flour

70g fresh white breadcrumbs

50g blanched almonds, roughly chopped

1 heaped tsp ground cinnamon

½–1 tsp ground allspice

½–1 tsp ground ginger

½ freshly grated nutmeg

A pinch of salt

3 eggs, beaten

Finely grated zest and juice of 1 lemon & 1 orange

Butter for greasing

The evening before you want to cook the pudding, you need to soak the fruit in the rum so it plumps up and softens. To help the process along a bit I put it into a warm cupboard where the central heating pipes run through. An airing cupboard would be good too, or the edge of an Aga if you are lucky enough to have one. Simply add all the dried fruit, along with the mixed peel, to a bowl, pour over the rum and mix well. Cover with clingfilm and rest in a warm place overnight.

The following day, mix the dry ingredients – the sugar, suet, flour, breadcrumbs and almonds – in a large bowl, along with all the spices and the salt. I tend to have a heavy hand when adding the spices. To me the essence of Christmas is captured in their heady scent, but go more lightly if you prefer.

In a small bowl, mix the egg with the orange and lemon juice and zest, then pour into the dry ingredients and mix well. Finally add the fruit and stir until well combined. At this point I make a wish or two for the year ahead, as was the family tradition when I was little. Wishes or no wishes, all the stirring allows a few moments of quiet reflection on the past, present and future.

Lightly grease a 2-pint pudding basin with a little butter, then pack in the pudding mixture. It will bulge over the top and you will think you can't get it all in, but you can – just! There is nothing worse than a stingy pudding. This one is designed to be well rounded to the point of voluptuousness.

Now for the slightly fiddly bit, wrapping the pudding ready for steaming. An extra pair of hands will make this job easier. Take a generous sheet of baking paper and fold a little pleat in the centre to allow for some expansion as the pudding cooks. Tie securely with a piece of string, then cover with a double sheet of foil.

Place an old saucer upside down in a large saucepan and rest the pudding on it. This takes the base of the pudding away from the heat source. Pour in enough boiling water to come halfway up the basin. Cover the saucepan tightly with a lid and simmer steadily over a medium heat for 6 hours, topping up with boiling water as necessary. Turn off the heat and allow the pudding to cool a little so you can lift it comfortably out of the pan.

Unwrap it, and slide a knife all around the inside to loosen the pudding, then invert the bowl on to a clean sheet of baking paper. Wrap the pudding first in the paper, then in a double layer of foil. Store in a cool dark cupboard until the big day.

To reheat the pudding, unwrap and put back into a lightly buttered pudding basin. Re-wrap the bowl as you did the first time – with a pleated piece of baking paper and a double layer of foil – and steam as before for 2 hours until warmed through. Invert on to a plate and serve piping hot with cream or brandy butter.

If you want to serve the pudding flaming, you need to get the brandy or rum really hot, so pour it into a deep ladle and heat over a gas flame. If you don't have a gas flame, heat it in a small saucepan. Hold the ladle over the pudding and light the surface of the alcohol with a match, then pour it over the pudding. Carefully carry the flaming pudding to the table to present with a flourish. Wait for the flames to die down before slicing and serving.

3rd December

Crème brûlée

PUDDING PERFECTION NOT TO BE MESSED WITH

This has to be one of my ultimate puddings. If I could only eat one more pudding in my life it might have to be this. A proper crème brûlée is divine. Made with just a handful of ingredients, it far exceeds the sum of its truly simple parts. While I am normally happy to experiment and play with ingredients in the kitchen, I'm afraid I'm a bit of a stickler for tradition in this case – not for me the tinkering with raspberries, chocolate or coffee that restaurants often try. Just cream, egg, vanilla and a little sugar. That's all. With something this simple, there is nowhere for the cook to hide – texture is everything and the beauty lies in the perfect balance between the luscious cool custard and the hard sweet crunch of the caramelized sugar surface.

While this is not a difficult thing to make, you do need to give it your full attention, stirring constantly as the vanilla-scented custard gradually thickens. It will take longer than you imagine, at least twenty minutes in my experience, but your patience will reap great rewards. Wander off to put the kettle on or answer the telephone and you risk everything. You have been warned.

Makes 4 individual puddings

600ml double cream	25g caster sugar
1 vanilla pod, split lengthways	3 tbsp Demerara sugar
6 egg yolks	

In a small, heavy-based saucepan, gradually warm the cream with the vanilla pod, stirring from time to time to release the seeds from the pod. As soon as the surface shows a suggestion of coming close to the boil, turn off the heat and let it infuse for 20 minutes.

Meanwhile, whisk together the egg yolks and caster sugar in a large roomy bowl until they thicken slightly. When the cream has infused, strain it through a sieve into the egg and sugar mixture. Beat together until thoroughly mixed then pour back into a clean pan. Have a whisk to hand. Warm the custard over the lowest possible heat, stirring constantly with a wooden spoon or heatproof silicone spatula. Every few minutes take the whisk and beat the custard firmly, then return to stirring. This disperses the heat, preventing hot spots, and distributes the thickening custard evenly through the mixture. Gradually the custard will thicken to an almost jelly-like wobble. While it must never reach boiling point, it needs to be taken pretty close, so be brave. If it looks to be getting too hot, remove the pan from the heat and whisk vigorously to cool a little before continuing.

Once you are happy it has thickened enough, pour into 4 ramekins and allow to cool. Then chill in the fridge for at least several hours, preferably overnight.

About half an hour before you want to serve them, scatter a fine layer of Demerara sugar over each. Don't be tempted to add too much as only the surface will melt and the underneath layer will remain unpleasantly gritty. I speak from experience. To caramelize the puddings you have two choices: either preheat an overhead grill to its very highest setting, or use a blow torch. I tend to use a blow torch as you can direct the heat to exactly where it needs to go. The idea is to melt and singe the sugar surface without overwarming the custard.

Return the crème brûlée to the fridge to chill again for 20 minutes or so before serving.

7th December

Yorkshire pudding with spring greens, sausages & caramelized shallot gravy

I love the idea of toad-in-the-hole, partly because of its child-friendly name, but I have always been a bit disappointed with the results. I have found it hard to get both the sausage and the batter crisp at the same time. So now I make a deconstructed version, where the sausage and the batter are cooked separately and then piled up on the plate. Served with a rich gravy and greens, this is just the hearty kind of dish you want for Sunday lunch or dinner on a cold winter's day. As we ate this I looked longingly out of the window to the raised beds, where my own cabbages were stubbornly failing to develop to a size worth harvesting. For now, a supermarket bag of spring greens sufficed. The chickens got the trimmings, for which they seemed chirpily grateful.

Serves 2 adults and 2 kids generously, for a family Sunday dinner

12 good quality chipolata sausages

400g shallots, peeled & cut into quarters

1 tbsp olive oil

2–3 sprigs fresh thyme

Freshly ground black pepper

2 heads of spring greens, shredded

A knob of butter

For the Yorkshire pudding:

225g plain flour

3 eggs

225ml milk

150ml water

1 tsp dried mixed herbs

Salt & freshly ground black pepper

3 tbsp olive oil

For the gravy:

1 tbsp plain flour

300ml beef or vegetable stock

75ml red wine (or extra stock)

Preheat the oven to 200°C/Gas 6.

Put the sausages and shallots in a sturdy roasting tin, drizzle over the olive oil and tuck in the thyme. Season with a little black pepper and toss to mix well. Roast in the middle of the oven for about 25 minutes until the sausages are cooked and the shallots are soft and lightly caramelized.

Make the Yorkshire pudding batter by whisking together the flour, eggs, milk, water, herbs and seasoning. Set aside.

About 10 minutes before the sausages are due to come out, pour the olive oil for the Yorkshire pudding into a roasting tray of about 25cm square. Place on the top shelf of the oven to heat up for 10 minutes.

Remove the sausages from the oven and transfer to a plate, along with the pieces of roast shallot, and wrap tightly in foil.

Remove the Yorkshire pudding tin from the oven and place over a low heat on the hob – it is important the oil stays as hot as possible. With a little care, pour the batter into the tin and get it back into the oven quickly. Cook until puffed up and golden, about 30 minutes.

Meanwhile, make the gravy in the sausage roasting tin by placing it over a low heat on the hob. Sprinkle in the flour and stir well, scraping at the bottom to release all the lovely caramelized bits. Pour in the stock and the wine, if using, stir through, then add the roast shallots. Bring up to a simmer and cook for 5 minutes. Taste to check the seasoning. You may want to add a little salt and some more black pepper.

Steam the greens until they are just tender. Drain and toss in a little butter. Serve the Yorkshire pudding cut into generous wedges, topped with the sausages and greens, then pour over the gravy.

9th December

Date, orange & pistachio bread & butter pudding

After a mild autumn, winter seems to have hit with a vengeance, and as usual the weather is having an impact on what I want to eat. Proper puddings seem to be the order of the day. No longer satisfied with a yogurt or piece of fruit, my body seems to demand something richer and more substantial. Today's bitterly chill wind and a lingering head cold meant I wanted to go nowhere further than a quick dash

to school and back, so pudding had to be constructed from what we already had. For me one of the most pleasurable things about cooking is a peek in the fridge, a rummage through the cupboards, followed by a good hard think about the possibilities. Born, I guess, from some sense of frugality and thrift, there is little nicer than creating something delicious out of nothing. No visits to the shop, no hunting for speciality ingredients, but something created from leftovers and bits and bobs. This bread and butter pudding was perhaps one of my best ever 'bits & bobs' dishes. I had none of the more usual raisins or currants, but I did have some dried dates that were right up against their best-before date. I had an orange, half a pot of cream, and of course I had eggs. And a rummage in the booze cupboard yielded a near-empty bottle of Cointreau left over from a cocktail party many moons ago. Only two tablespoons, but enough to lift this pudding from the gorgeous to the sublime. Oh yes, I was really rather pleased with this.

Serves 4

100g dried dates, roughly chopped

Finely grated zest and juice of 1 large orange

250ml milk

150ml double cream

3 eggs

2 tbsp orange liqueur, such as Cointreau (optional)

9 slices good quality white bread, crusts trimmed – slightly stale is best (about 250g without crusts)

30–40g butter, plus extra for greasing

100g shell-on pistachios, yielding about 50g nuts, roughly chopped

2–3 tbsp Demerara sugar

In a small saucepan, simmer the dates in the orange juice for a couple of minutes, then turn off and leave to infuse for a few minutes while you make the custard. Mix together the orange zest with the milk, cream, eggs, and liqueur if you are using it. Stir the dates and orange juice into the custard mixture.

Generously butter the bread, cut it into wedges or triangles depending on the shape of your loaf, and arrange half in a lightly greased baking dish. I used thin slices from a large flat, round 'boule'-type bread. It had plenty of air holes which made wonderful pockets for the custard to puddle in. Pour over half the custard, then top with the remaining bread, followed by the rest of the custard. Leave to soak for around 30 minutes before cooking.

Preheat the oven to 180°C/Gas 4.

When you are ready to cook, evenly sprinkle over the shelled and roughly chopped pistachios and the Demerara sugar. Bake for around 30–35 minutes until the custard has just set but still has a slight wobble to it, and the surface is crisp and golden.

Serve warm from the oven. I found it rich enough to eat on its own, but you may want to offer a little extra cream alongside.

17th December

Spiced nut meringues with Marsala cream

Old friends were coming for dinner and I wanted to make a pudding that was a little bit Christmassy but without being too in-your-face festive. There would be enough of that in the coming days. Meringues are a really useful thing to make when you have people coming over. They keep well for a few days, so no last-minute slaving in the kitchen. I made these with some leftover egg white I had frozen a couple of weeks previously. Before I kept chickens and found myself with a pretty much constant glut of eggs, I had no idea that eggs can be frozen so successfully. I freeze them, the white and yolk separately, in ice cube trays, then I knock them out and put the cubes in a bag. You then have access to a small quantity of both – very useful when you just need a little to glaze a pie or seal up some sausage rolls. With meringues, the golden rule is twice the weight of sugar to egg white.

Makes 6 large meringues

For the spiced nuts:

1 egg white

2 tbsp golden caster sugar

1 tsp ground cinnamon

1 tsp ground mixed spice

½ tsp ground ginger

½ tsp ground mace

200g mixed nuts (I used a combination of walnuts, almonds & hazelnuts)

For the meringues:

3 egg whites

200g golden caster sugar (or double the weight of the egg whites)

For the Marsala cream:

300ml double cream

1 tbsp icing sugar

Approx. 50ml Marsala, to taste

Preheat the oven to 180°C/Gas 4.

For the spiced nuts, put the egg white in a small bowl and stir through the golden caster sugar and spices until you have a thick paste. Add the nuts and toss well to coat all over. Spread out in a single layer on a baking tray lined with baking paper and roast in the oven for 10 minutes. Remove and allow to cool a little, then roughly chop.

Reduce the oven heat to 110°C/Gas ¼, leaving the door ajar so it cools quicker.

Weigh the remaining egg whites into a clean bowl. Whatever the weight of egg white, use twice the amount of sugar. My eggs needed 195g of sugar but yours might differ. Whisk the egg white until it is thick and fluffy, then add half the sugar and whisk until well incorporated. Add the rest of the sugar and whisk again until the meringue is thick and glossy. Fold through about half the chopped nuts.

Divide the meringue into 6 even dollops on 2 baking trays lined with non-stick paper – 3 per tray – allowing plenty of space between each as they will grow in the oven. Flatten each dollop out, making a shallow dip in the middle that will be filled with the cream. Bake for about 2 hours until they lift cleanly and easily off the baking paper. Allow to cool.

In a large bowl, whisk the cream with the icing sugar until thickened a little. Add the Marsala to taste and continue to whisk until whipped. Store in the fridge until you are ready to serve – it will sit quite happily for a few hours.

To serve, spoon the cream into the centre of each meringue and scatter over the rest of the nuts.

23rd December

Festive rabbit & prune pâté

Not a particularly 'eggy' recipe this one, using just one of them to bind the pâté together, but we have such a constant supply that any dish that uses them is a good thing. And besides, I don't think Christmas would be Christmas without some sort of pâté in the house, and the joy of home-made is you know exactly what's gone into it. I like to flavour mine intensely with plenty of herbs, spices and alcohol. This one used a whole rabbit that I bought on a whim when I was at the butcher's picking up my festive order. I often think we should try to be a bit less squeamish about eating rabbit. The wild ones have led a truly free-range life and, being such proficient breeders, they are a sustainable source of protein.

Like all pâté, this is best made a few days before you want to serve it. The flavours will mature beautifully – today's will be perfection by Boxing Day. Pâté also freezes well. I cut my block in

half, putting one lot in the fridge while the other, well wrapped in baking paper, went into the freezer for a delicious savoury treat at a later date.

Makes 1 loaf tin, serving 8–10

1 fresh rabbit, skinned & gutted	100ml port
50g unsalted butter	12 prunes, roughly chopped
1 onion, chopped	1 egg
2–3 cloves garlic, sliced	2 bay leaves, finely sliced
1 tbsp olive oil	½ tsp ground mace
250g chicken livers	Sea salt & freshly ground black pepper
100g fatty pancetta, smoked if possible	

Prepare the rabbit by using a small sharp knife to remove as much of the flesh from the body and legs as possible. Set the meat aside. You can roast the bones with carrot, onion, celery and herbs to make a delicious base for a stock or gravy, as I did in preparation for my Christmas Day feast.

In a large frying pan, melt the butter over a low heat, add the onion and garlic and sweat until soft and translucent. The longer and more gently you cook the onions and garlic, the sweeter they become, so don't rush this step. Expect to be cooking them for around 30 minutes. Using a slotted spoon (leaving behind as much of the butter as possible), transfer the cooked onions and garlic to a food processor.

Add the olive oil to the pan – this will help stop the butter burning when you fry the meat. Turn up the heat and fry the rabbit meat, chicken livers and pancetta in batches until golden brown. Don't overcrowd the pan or the meat will sweat rather than fry and you will lose a valuable flavour opportunity. Transfer each batch of meat to the processor bowl as it is done.

Add the port to the frying pan and deglaze, taking the time to scrape the sticky caramelized bits off the bottom. Pour the pan juices into the processor, along with the prunes, egg, bay leaves and mace, and blitz to a coarse purée. Season well with black pepper and sea salt. As pâté is served cold, I find you need to be quite generous with the salt despite the salty pancetta – cold foods need much more vigorous seasoning than hot.

Preheat the oven to 180°/Gas 4.

Pour the pâté into a large (2lb) well-greased loaf tin. Cover in a double layer of baking paper, and finish with a tight layer of foil. Lower into a deep roasting dish and pour in enough boiling water to come halfway up the tin. Cook in the oven for 1 1/4 hours, after which time the pâté should be starting to come away from the edges of the tin a little. Remove from the oven and weigh down the top to compress the pâté as it cools. I find a couple of well-balanced tins of baked beans do this job adequately, if a little precariously.

Once the pâté is cool, run a knife around the edge of the tin and invert on to a board. A sharp tap should release the pâté.

25th December

Scrambled egg with smoked salmon

TRADITIONAL CHRISTMAS DAY BREAKFAST

I admit I was unsure whether to write a recipe for plain old scrambled egg, especially as there is a slightly more exotic tomato and cheese version on page 153. But as it is something of a weekend family ritual, one we go through several times a month, I do feel I've learned a thing or two about how to make it. On Christmas Day we always, always have it for breakfast, normally with slices of smoked salmon as a way to keep us all going, through a wintry dog walk and beyond, until Christmas dinner is ready in the late afternoon.

I start by cracking a rather generous three eggs per person (two for the kids) into a bowl and whisking them lightly with a fork, seasoning with plenty of salt and freshly ground black pepper as I go. Many recipes call for only two eggs each, but I figure if you're having eggs for breakfast you may as well do it properly. Then I add a large knob of butter, always unsalted as it burns less easily, to a heavy-based pan and allow it to melt slowly over a low to medium heat. I tend to favour a lovely sturdy copper pan from a set that Mum bought me and Rob as a wedding present. Now a decade old, they are used on an almost daily basis.

Once the butter has melted, in go the seasoned eggs. Then I leave them alone for 30 seconds or so before giving them a thorough stir with a heatproof spatula. I don't like them too smooth, so I don't stir continuously but follow a cycle of leave-them, then-stir-them, until they are two-thirds of the way to being set. At this point, turn off the heat and let them finish by themselves. Then eat as quickly as possible.

27th December

Christmas ham, egg & salsa verde sandwich

On Christmas Eve I found myself simmering a large joint of ham, ludicrous really as we weren't expecting masses of people over the holidays, but it felt like a nice Christmassy thing to do and filled the house with lovely seasonal aromas. A few days later we finally carved into it for lunch and, teamed with a punchy salsa verde and

soft-boiled eggs, it made a very pleasant change from the cheese, pâté and sausage rolls we had been living on during the days previous.

I love salsa verde, literally 'green sauce', probably more even than home-made pesto. Its vibrant colour is equally matched by its bold piquant flavours and it is the perfect thing to liven up lentils, salads, cold meat or fish. This sauce is all about balancing the flavours, so it is essential to taste as you go. You are looking for the perfect balance of salty and sweet and herby. Your perfect balance will be different to mine so trust your own judgement on this one and use my recipe only as a guide. The texture, too, is a personal matter. My preference is for a relatively smooth sauce. Process it less if you want it more rustic. It will keep in the fridge for a few days; press down the surface of the salsa verde with a layer of clingfilm to stop it oxidizing.

Serves 4 for lunch, with extra sauce

Generous bunch of flat-leaf parsley, roughly torn

Small bunch of mint, roughly torn

Small bunch of chives, roughly torn

1 clove garlic, coarsely chopped

1 tbsp Dijon mustard

2–3 tbsp capers

3–4 cornichons (small gherkins)

3–4 salted anchovy fillets

Juice of ½–1 lemon

1–2 tsp caster sugar

100–150ml extra virgin olive oil

Salt & freshly ground black pepper

4 eggs

Butter (optional)

4 slices thick-cut rustic bread

4 slices thick-cut ham or gammon

For the salsa verde, put the herbs, garlic and mustard into a food processor and pulse until roughly combined. Then add the capers, cornichons, anchovy fillets, lemon juice and sugar, starting with a little of each, and pulse to a paste, loosening the sauce with the olive oil. Taste as you go and add a little more of what you fancy. Season with salt and black pepper.

Put the eggs in a pan of cold water, covering them by a

centimetre or so. Bring up to a gentle simmer and cook for 4 minutes to give you a set white and a runny yolk. Cook for a minute or so longer if you prefer a harder yolk. Run under cold water for a minute until cool enough to handle, then peel.

Assemble the sandwich, buttering the bread if you like, with the ham on the bottom, the eggs cut in half and drizzled generously with salsa verde on top. Eat while the eggs are still warm.

31st December

Three ices for New Year's Eve

Never known for my under-catering, I decide to make not one but three different ices for a celebratory pudding for friends coming round on New Year's Eve. This is in part, I admit, to use up the gallon of cream I have in the fridge – leftovers from an overzealous pre-Christmas shop. But it is also to satisfy my need to place something generous and ample on the table when feeding those I care about. You could very well make some biscuits to nibble alongside, such as the almond thins on page 257. I didn't, as I felt that to be a step too far, considering the feast that went before.

Ice cream is always easier and better – smoother, creamier – if you churn it in an ice-cream machine. I have used the same machine for over a decade, a very cheap and cheerful one where you store the bowl in the freezer so it's ready when you need it. I did once consider a more expensive model that both freezes and churns, but frankly mine works very well and I am loath to get rid of it. If you don't possess an ice-cream maker, simply freeze in a shallow dish, mixing and stirring several times during the freezing process to break up the ice crystals. It will still taste lovely but the texture won't be quite as refined.

Sorbet, on the other hand, I don't make in my ice-cream maker. I find that the egg white, which is added to soften the texture, doesn't really combine properly this way – it seems to need more vigorous measures. So I pour it into a container and freeze it solid, then scrape it into a food processor and whizz for a few seconds to break up the ice crystals. Then I put it back into the freezer to set again.

Like all ices, these are best allowed to thaw a little before being served, so take them out of the freezer and put in the fridge an hour or so ahead of time.

Bitter chocolate & cardamom

Be warned, this is a very strong, very rich ice cream and probably not one that will become a favourite with the kids. Which is fine in my book, home-made ice cream is far too nice to save for children alone. If you have an aversion to cardamom, leave it out, but I would urge you to try it – the spice imparts a subtle, smoky and quite unique taste that will get your guests talking.

Makes about 500ml

12 cardamom pods

350ml milk

150ml double cream

150g dark chocolate (70% cocoa solids)

30g cocoa powder

125g soft brown sugar

4 egg yolks

Lightly crush the cardamom pods so they crack open to reveal the little black seeds inside. Reserve 2 of the pods, adding the rest to a small heavy-based pan, along with the milk and cream. Heat gently until just below boiling point, then turn off the heat and leave to infuse for 1 hour.

Melt the chocolate in a bowl set over a pan of barely simmering water. Add the cocoa powder and sugar and stir well to combine. Remove from the heat and allow to cool. Once cool, stir in the egg yolks, then pour over the cream, mixing really well. Pour into a clean saucepan and warm very gently over the lowest flame possible, stirring pretty much constantly. After a while, 10 minutes or so, the custard will start to thicken. Keep cooking for another few minutes until it reaches the consistency of thick cream. Pour into a clean bowl, press down a layer of clingfilm on the surface to stop a skin forming, and allow to cool.

Take the black seeds out of the remaining cardamom pods and crush to a powder with a pestle and mortar. Stir through the cooled chocolate custard, then put in the fridge to chill for several hours, overnight if possible.

Once thoroughly chilled, churn in an ice-cream maker according to the manufacturer's instructions.

Tonka bean ice cream

Tonka beans make the most interesting and amazingly decadent ice cream. *What* beans, I hear you cry! Well, they are a rather weird and wonderful ingredient from South America that I stumbled upon when they had been used to flavour a perfect crème brûlée I ate at a restaurant in Bristol. One taste and I knew I had to track them down for a culinary experiment. They look a bit like large dried rabbit droppings, and you grate them as you would a nutmeg. The aroma is rather difficult to describe, a little like smoky spiced almonds, perhaps tinged with just a *touch* of cyanide essence. Joking aside, they are really rather strange and quite tricky to get hold of, but very well worth it. I bought my little jar online, at a spice supplier called Steenbergs.

Makes about 500ml

300ml double cream

200ml milk

1½ tonka beans, finely grated

5 egg yolks

125g golden caster sugar

Put the cream and milk in a small, heavy-based saucepan and stir in the grated tonka bean. Bring up to the boil, turn the heat down to a simmer and allow to bubble gently for 5 minutes. Remove from the heat and leave to infuse for an hour or two.

Whisk together the egg yolks and sugar in a roomy bowl until thick and glossy. Strain over the tonka-infused cream and whisk together. Pour into a clean saucepan, set over the lowest heat possible and gently warm, stirring all the time until it starts to thicken. Allow to cook until it is the consistency of double cream. Pour into a bowl and press the surface with a layer of clingfilm. Allow to cool, then chill for several hours or overnight. Freeze in your ice-cream maker following the manufacturer's instructions.

Orange flower water sorbet

Makes about 500ml

Finely grated zest of 2 oranges

500ml freshly squeezed orange juice, about 5–8 oranges

200g caster sugar

1 egg white

2 tbsp orange flower water

Put the orange zest and half the orange juice into a small pan along with the sugar. Bring to a gentle simmer and stir for a couple of minutes until the sugar has dissolved. Remove from the heat and allow to cool.

In a large bowl, whisk the egg white until frothy and thick. Pour in the orange sugar syrup, the remaining orange juice and the orange flower water. Whisk together as thoroughly as you can – the egg white will be a bit reluctant – then pour into a container and freeze until solid. When it has pretty much set, scrape into a food processor and pulse for a few seconds to break up the ice crystals. Pour back into the container and refreeze.

1st January

Simple citrus drizzle cake

THE FIRST CAKE OF THE NEW YEAR

The weekend, as has become the tradition in our house, saw the need to bake a cake. The first cake of the new year, for me, had to be a super simple affair, especially considering the party of the night before. Not hugely wild, but wild enough, and the kids as usual were up at 7 a.m. I was not looking for a fudgy fancy confection of chocolate or gooey icing but something satisfying to go with a cup of tea. A quick glance at the less than impressive post-Christmas fruit bowl gave me instant inspiration: 2 rapidly yellowing limes, a slightly soft lemon, a large, not-bad-looking orange and a very much past-it melon. The melon was quartered and given to the chickens – who devoured it in a matter of minutes – as a small way of thanking them for their part in the cake-making process. The rest of the fruit were to be turned into a citrus drizzle cake, sharp yet sweet, simple and pure. My idea of cake nirvana, and somehow perfectly right for the first, slightly foggy-of-mind, Sunday of the year.

Cuts into about 8 slices

3 eggs, separated

180g unsalted butter, plus extra for greasing

180g caster sugar

160g self-raising flour

60g ground almonds

Finely grated zest of 2 limes, 1 lemon and 1 orange (reserve the juice)

3 tbsp milk

For the syrup:

The citrus juice from above

100g caster sugar

Preheat the oven to 200°C/Gas 6. Grease and line a large (2lb) loaf tin with a strip of baking paper, leaving a 'tail' at either end to help you lift the cake out.

Either in a food mixer with a whisk attachment, or in a roomy bowl with an electric whisk, whisk up the egg whites until stiff. Be sure that both the bowl and whisk are super-clean before you start as any hint of grease can mean the whites will not gain enough air to fluff up. Once the egg whites are whisked, set aside.

In a separate bowl, add the egg yolks, butter and sugar and beat together until light and fluffy. I used the beater attachment of my food mixer, as I tend to be a lazy cake-maker, especially with a post-New Year's Eve hangover. Beat in the flour, ground almonds and all of the citrus zest, and finally beat in the milk.

Take a generous spoon of the whisked egg white and beat this into the cake mixture; this will serve to loosen it a little. Then fold the remaining egg whites in gently but firmly, taking care not to over-mix or you will lose the precious air you spent time whisking in.

Pour into the prepared tin, levelling slightly with the back of a spoon, and cook in the oven until a skewer inserted into the centre comes out clean, about 40–45 minutes.

While the cake is cooking, prepare the 'drizzle' by boiling the reserved citrus juice and the sugar in a small saucepan. Remove from the heat when the sugar has dissolved and you are left with a glossy syrup that tastes quite sharp. If you want it sweeter, add a little more sugar, but for me the drizzle should have a zing that tingles on the tongue and serves to wake the cake up, lifting it from the plain to the zestily sublime.

Once the cake is done, remove it from the oven and, while it is still hot, slowly pour the drizzle over. Do this spoonful by spoonful, and watch it satisfyingly soak into the sponge. Don't rush or it will puddle and run over the sides of the tin, which would be a shameful waste of the delicious nectar. Allow to cool in the tin before lifting out on to a plate and serving.

7th January

Eve's pudding

The first fine and clear day of the year was spent in the garden, planting ferns in a shady corner and sweeping up a multitude of fallen leaves outside the back door. The weak sun served to lift my spirits and reminded me that spring was just around the corner. So close I swear I could almost smell it. That's optimism for you.

Eve's pudding is an old English classic where slices of apple are baked under a layer of light sponge. Simple, comforting and really quick to make, to my mind this is far easier than a crumble or a pie. I made this in honour of Eve, my beautiful, strong-willed daughter, aged four, who was thrilled to have a pudding named after her. Infuriatingly, she then refused to eat it, announcing raw apples to be fine and delicious, whereas cooked apples are not.

I know many people see January as a month to detox and trim down after the excesses of Christmas. But to me it is *the* month of the year when I need to nourish my soul and feed my body. My concession to healthy eating was to be a touch heavy on the quantity of apples and slim on the sponge. This would be wonderful served with the custard on page 163, but I wasn't in a custard-making mood so a dribble of single cream had to suffice. And perfect it was too.

Serves 4

For the filling:

800g Bramley apples (about 3–4 medium)

50g golden caster sugar

½ lemon

A little butter, for greasing

For the sponge:

120g golden caster sugar

120g unsalted butter

120g self-raising flour

2 eggs

3 tbsp milk

1 tbsp Demerara sugar (optional, but gives a lovely, slightly crunchy top)

Preheat the oven to 180°C/Gas 4. Lightly grease an ovenproof dish.

Peel and core the apples, then slice thinly, no thicker than a pound coin. Scatter half in an even layer over the base of the dish. Sprinkle over about half the sugar and squeeze over a little lemon juice.

Add the remaining apple, the rest of the sugar and another squeeze of lemon. Set aside while you make the sponge.

The sponge couldn't be easier. Simply put all the ingredients (except the Demerara sugar) into a food processor and whizz until evenly combined. An electric whisk or food mixer would be a good alternative. You are looking for a batter that drops easily from a spoon. Spread the batter evenly over the apples and sprinkle over the Demerara sugar.

Bake for around 45 minutes until deep golden brown. Pierce with a skewer to test. The apple should be soft and the cake cooked. Best served warm rather than hot, with cream or custard.

10th January

Kedgeree with poached eggs
INAUTHENTIC BUT NEVERTHELESS DELICIOUS

What a dismal day. It felt like it never really got light. We were shrouded in drizzly gloom from dawn to dusk. The chickens seemed to deal with it just fine, happily grubbing about all day long. I fared less well, and felt pretty low and out of sorts. What I needed to cheer me up was a wonderfully warm and comforting supper. Mildly spiced, carbohydrate-rich and subtly smoky, kedgeree seemed to be ticking all my boxes. And what better way to serve it than topped with a wonderfully fresh egg from the garden, poached to perfection?

Serves 2, generously

350–400g smoked haddock fillet, preferably undyed

50g unsalted butter

2 bay leaves

250ml milk (whole or semi)

Freshly ground black pepper

1 leek, washed & finely sliced

1 tsp each of cumin seeds & coriander seeds

½ tsp turmeric powder

3 cardamom pods, lightly bruised

150g basmati rice

Approx. 200ml stock (vegetable or chicken)

2 generous handfuls spinach leaves, washed & drained

Sea salt

1 tsp white wine vinegar

2 eggs, as fresh as possible

Loose handful of flat-leaf parsley, roughly chopped

Preheat the oven to 180°C/Gas 4. Lay the fish in a snug single layer in a baking dish and dot with half the butter. Add the bay leaves, pour over the milk and season generously with freshly ground black pepper, but no salt at this stage as smoked haddock can be quite salty. Cover tightly with foil and bake in the oven for about 25 minutes, or until the fish is just cooked through – this could vary a little depending on the thickness of the fillet so keep an eye on it.

While the fish is cooking, add the remaining butter to a heavy-based saucepan and melt over a low heat. Add the leek and cook very gently until soft – about 10 minutes. An even slightly burnt leek is a bitter thing, so take care. To facilitate gentle cooking I take a piece of baking paper and scrunch it up into a ball under running water, then unscrunch it and lay it over the leeks, tucking it slightly under at the sides. This creates a damp steamy lid and stops the pan getting too hot.

In a small, dry frying pan, toast the spices for no more than a minute, then coarsely grind with a pestle and mortar. This may seem like a faff, but it wakes up the spices and makes all the difference. Add the spices to the leeks and fry for another 1–2 minutes – this time without the paper lid, which you can discard. Add the rice and stir well to coat in the spiced buttery juices.

Remove the fish from the oven and carefully drain off the milk into a jug. Top up with the stock to give about 450ml liquid, and pour over the rice. I used chicken stock as I had it in the fridge. It worked fine and tasted great, but vegetable stock would be the more obvious choice. Bring up to the boil, stir well and cover with a tight-fitting lid. Turn the heat as low as possible and simmer for 10 minutes, resisting the urge to peek.

Flake the fish carefully, checking for any little bones, and set aside in a warm place – back into the cooling oven is ideal.

After 10 minutes, add the spinach to the rice. Don't stir but leave as a deep green, leafy layer on top. Cover and cook for 2 more minutes, until wilted. Gently fold it through the rice, along with the flaked fish, and taste to check the seasoning. Now is the time to add a little salt, and possibly more pepper. Turn off the heat, cover and leave to rest while you poach the eggs.

Fill a wide, deep frying pan with cold water and bring to the boil. Add the vinegar, turn the heat down to a gentle simmer, and carefully crack the eggs into the water. Leave pretty much undisturbed until they are done to your liking. For a yolk that is not too runny, not too dry: about 4 minutes. For a runnier yolk: 3 minutes. A good way to check is to touch the surface of the yolk gently with your finger to see how much 'give' it has. The more give, the softer the yolk still is.

Serve the kedgeree in warm bowls, topped with an egg and scattered with the parsley.

13th January

Coffee custard & bananas

A GROWN-UP COMFORT PUDDING

Banana custard was a schooldays favourite, but at home Mum went one stage better than plain old custard – coffee custard. Logic tells me that coffee and bananas shouldn't work together, but somehow they do, they really do. In the 1970s coffee custard could only mean one thing – Camp coffee essence mixed into Bird's custard powder. I can still taste it now. It was a delicious, genius invention and something I have been longing to recreate for years. So tonight it was to be home-made coffee custard, made with proper coffee, to serve poured over sliced bananas. A retro grown-up comfort pudding, just the thing for a Friday night on the sofa, fire blazing.

You could turn this custard very easily into coffee ice cream by churning it, once cool, in an ice-cream maker. The only alteration I'd make is to add a little more sugar, just another 30g or so. The colder things are, the less sweet they seem. Frozen puddings need to be almost cloyingly sweet in their unfrozen state; once solid, they taste just right.

Enough for 2 greedy people in need of a treat

4 egg yolks	100ml single cream
60g caster sugar	2 tbsp very strong coffee
200ml milk	2 bananas, cut into slices

In a glass bowl, whisk the egg yolks with the sugar until slightly thickened. Set aside.

Pour the milk and cream into a heavy-based saucepan and heat gently until just below boiling point. Keep an eagle eye on it: milk is infuriatingly susceptible to exploding over the top of the pan. As it begins to bubble up, pour it into the bowl with the egg and sugar, whisking all the time until completely combined, then add the coffee and whisk again. Wash the pan, pour the custard back in and heat over the lowest setting, stirring constantly, until it thickens to the consistency of double cream. Be patient, this will take at least 10 minutes. Don't be tempted to turn up the heat or you will risk separation and curdling. Should it look like you have overstepped the mark, remove the custard from the heat and whisk as hard as you can. If the worst comes to the worst and it has split, an energetic blast in the blender usually rescues it. (I hope you won't need to test this.)

Now you have a decision to make. Hot coffee custard, or cold coffee custard? My preference is for cold, not ice cold, but chilly room-temperature cold. So I pour it into a bowl and leave it, clingfilm pressed on top to stop a skin forming, until it is cold. And only then do I pour it over my sliced banana.

15th January

Cheese gougères with creamed leeks & cider-braised gammon

A gougère is a rather fancy-sounding name for a choux pastry that is enriched with strong cheese. Choux is more often eaten as a sweet pastry in profiteroles and éclairs, but this savoury version makes a good alternative to a Yorkshire pudding. The richness of the cheese means the pastry doesn't puff up quite as much as sweet choux, but it tastes great. I used bread flour in my recipe. It gives a slightly crisper result than ordinary flour. But if you don't have any, use plain flour instead.

I often cook a ham for Sunday lunch. It makes a nice change from

roast chicken, and best of all is its usefulness in midweek cooking. Leftovers from a generous joint will be turned into sandwiches, quick pasta or risotto dishes, or just generally nibbled.

Serves 4, with plenty of leftover ham

For the gammon:

1.5–2kg gammon piece, smoked or unsmoked

1.5 litres dry cider

2 carrots, roughly chopped

1 onion, roughly chopped

1 stick of celery, roughly chopped

6 whole black peppercorns

6 cloves

2 bay leaves

For the gougère:

120g strong plain (bread) flour

A pinch of ground mace

Salt & freshly ground black pepper

300ml cold water

100g unsalted butter

4 eggs

100g strong Cheddar, grated

For the creamed leeks:

4 medium leeks, finely sliced & thoroughly washed under running water

300ml double cream

A few sage leaves, very finely chopped

Salt & freshly ground black pepper

Put the gammon in a large saucepan and pour over the cider. Add the carrots, onion, celery, peppercorns, cloves and bay leaves, and top up with a little water if necessary to ensure the gammon is just submerged. Bring up to the boil then reduce the heat to a steady simmer, cover the pan loosely with a lid or foil and cook for 2 hours. I tend to serve the ham simply boiled; I find it is more succulent like this. But if you prefer, you could lift it from the cooking juices, brush with a little honey and put it into a hot oven for 15–20 minutes to glaze it.

When the ham is nearly cooked, begin the gougère. Preheat the oven to 200°C/Gas 6. Sift the flour into a bowl, sprinkle over the mace and season with a little salt and black pepper. Leave it ready by the hob. Measure the water into a saucepan and add the butter, setting over a medium heat. Once the butter has melted and the water is boiling, turn off the heat and quickly add the flour all in one go, stirring briskly until you have a smooth ball of paste. This takes only half a minute or so. Set aside to cool for 10 minutes.

Break the eggs into a jug and lightly beat them. Add the egg to the cooled mixture, a little at a time, beating well between each addition until you have a smooth and glossy paste. Beat in the cheese until evenly distributed.

At this point take 2 baking trays and cut 2 sheets of baking paper to fit. Run the baking paper under a cold tap to wet it then shake off the excess and lay the sheets on the trays. The damp paper helps to create a steamy atmosphere that in turn helps the gougère to rise. Using a tablespoon, make even-sized mounds on each baking tray, spacing them well apart so they have room to spread. Bake in the hot oven for 25 minutes, after which time they should have puffed up and turned a deep golden brown.

While the gougères are in the oven, blanch the leeks in boiling water for 4–5 minutes until just tender. Drain really well then return to the pan, along with the cream and sage. Simmer gently for 5 minutes, seasoning to taste with a little salt and black pepper.

Carve the ham into thick slices and serve with the leeks spooned over and the gougères on the side. A smear of English mustard would be a very welcome accompaniment.

20th January

Chocolate & walnut torte

I am no chocoholic. Chocolate is something I can generally take or leave. But there are occasions when only a slice of chocolate cake will do, and this is a great one, very chocolatey and dense, and very useful – it will last happily in a tin for several days without drying out or going stale. I used to make a similar cake but with ground almonds instead of walnuts, but this is far, far better. In my mind, no other nut offers the complexity in flavour that walnuts do, and they seem to have a natural affinity with chocolate.

It is not a frugal cake. It uses a whole pack of butter, and quite a few bowls in the making, but it is worth it. It is very rich and will easily serve ten or so people as a small slice is plenty. You can make it entirely without flour if you want to serve it as a gluten-free cake, but the flour offers some stability to the mix. Without it, it is likely to be a little more fragile and may crack as it cools. But it will still taste delicious.

Serves 10 generously

300g good quality dark chocolate (preferably 70% cocoa solids), broken into pieces

250g unsalted butter, plus extra for greasing the tin

250g walnut pieces

4 eggs, separated

200g caster sugar

1 tsp vanilla extract

50g plain flour

Preheat the oven to 160°C/Gas 3. Prepare a 23cm springform tin by lining the base with baking paper and greasing the sides with a little butter.

Set a bowl over a pan of barely simmering water, making sure the base doesn't come into contact with the water. Add half the chocolate and the butter and melt slowly, taking care not to let it get too hot.

Place the walnuts in a food processor and blitz until finely ground. Add the other half of the chocolate and pulse until chopped into little pieces.

In a large roomy bowl, whisk the egg yolks with the sugar and vanilla extract until thick and pale. Pour in the melted butter and chocolate and mix well, followed by the ground walnuts and chocolate and the flour. Beat well together.

In a separate bowl, whisk the egg whites until stiff. Using a large metal spoon, fold the egg whites into the cake mixture, cutting through in a figure-of-eight shape to minimize air loss.

Pour into the prepared tin, gently levelling the surface with the flat of a knife. Bake in the oven for about 50 minutes or until a skewer comes out pretty much clean – bearing in mind you may pierce a piece of molten chocolate. This is the sort of dense cake that would benefit from being very slightly under- rather than over-cooked.

22nd January

Nasi goreng with nam prik sauce

Many years ago I was lucky enough to go to Indonesia and Malaysia several times for work. I completely fell in love with the sweet, hot and salty food there. This is my cuisine of choice when I feel the need for a bit of chilli in my life. Which happens often, to the point where I think I might have a mild, but ultimately pretty harmless, addiction. Egg and chilli have such a natural affinity, and in Indonesia the rice is either topped with a fried egg or sometimes wrapped up parcel-like in a thin omelette. I prefer the fried egg option as it is a little less faffy. To me, this dish of spicy Indonesian fried rice is the perfect lazy night sofa-supper, fire blazing and telly on.

I first came across the delicious but fiery nam prik sauce in Rick Stein's excellent book *Far Eastern Odyssey*. This recipe has been adapted and tweaked from his over the making of many batches in order to get it just how I like it. It is very, very intense, and your eyes will water when you make it, but it is really worth it. You need just a little for this dish but it will keep, unopened, for months provided you have sterilized your jars. Once you open a jar, store it in the fridge and use within six weeks or so.

To sterilize jars and lids, wash well in soapy water then rinse. Shake off excess water and line up on a baking tray. Place in the oven at 160°C/Gas 3 and allow to dry completely: about 20 minutes. Once sterile, don't touch the inside of the lids or jars.

Serves 2

For the nam prik sauce – makes 3 small jars (of about 190g each):

120g dried chilli flakes

40g shrimp paste

150ml vegetable oil

50g dried shrimps

200g shallots, chopped

1 bulb garlic, cloves peeled & finely chopped

75g jaggery (palm sugar) or soft brown sugar

65g seedless tamarind pulp

2 tbsp fish sauce

For the nasi goreng:

120g basmati or jasmine rice

100ml vegetable oil

1 large onion, finely sliced

2 cloves garlic, sliced

3cm fresh ginger, grated

2 tsp nam prik sauce

2 tbsp kecap manis (Indonesian sweet soy sauce), or dark soy plus a tsp of caster sugar

1 tbsp tomato ketchup

2 handfuls cavolo nero or spring greens finely sliced (about 100g)

125g chestnut mushrooms, sliced

100g frozen peas

200g raw king prawns, cut in half

Salt

2 eggs, plus a little vegetable oil for frying

To make the nam prik sauce, tip the dried chilli flakes into a wok and dry-fry for a minute or two. They will be very pungent and your eyes will water as they get hot. Tip into a spice mill, in batches if necessary, and grind to a coarse powder, adding each batch to the bowl of a food processor as it is done.

Wrap the shrimp paste in a sheet of foil to make a small parcel. Add to the wok and fry, pressing down with a spatula, for a minute on each side. Remove and allow to cool a little before unwrapping and scraping into the food processor. Next, add the oil to the wok and fry the dried shrimps until crisp and golden. Remove with a slotted spoon and add to the processor. Add the shallots and fry until crisp and golden, then remove them to the processor. Finally, fry the garlic until golden then add, along with all the oil, to the processor. Whiz everything together to form a thin paste, then scrape back into the wok. Add the jaggery or brown sugar, tamarind pulp and fish sauce, and stir over a low heat. Allow the sauce to thicken and bubble for about 5 minutes, stirring regularly to prevent it sticking. Spoon into hot sterilized jars and seal tightly.

To make the nasi goreng, cook the rice according to the packet instructions (or see my method on page 28) then drain and rinse under plenty of cold running water until cold. Set aside.

Put the oil in a wok and fry the onion until crisp and deep golden brown. Remove with a slotted spoon on to kitchen paper to drain. Discard all but a tablespoon of oil, then fry the garlic for a couple of minutes until lightly golden. Add the ginger, nam prik, kecap manis (or soy and sugar) and ketchup, and stir-fry for a minute. Toss in the greens, mushrooms and peas and stir-fry for 4–5 minutes until just tender. Add the prawns and continue to stir-fry until they are pink and cooked all the way through, a matter of 2–3 minutes. Finally stir the rice through, cook until hot and season to taste with a little salt.

Fry the eggs in a separate pan until they are cooked to your liking. Serve the rice in deep bowls topped with an egg, the fried onions and possibly another smear of nam prik on top.

28th January

Baghdad eggs with herb yogurt & pitta crisps

Baghdad eggs, also known as Turkish eggs, are spiced fried eggs with punchy Middle-Eastern flavours. They made for a fresh and interesting brunch dish, and they were a welcome change from the more usual scrambled or poached. Eggs go so well with herbs and spices and this dish used both in abundance.

Pitta crisps are easy and delicious, and so useful that I often make a double or even treble batch. They store well in an airtight tin for a week or two, or even longer if you crisp them back up for a few minutes in a hot oven, and are great with all manner of dips or just for snacking on when you feel peckish. So much tastier and healthier than reaching for a bag of regular crisps. I normally add chilli flakes because I can't resist the opportunity to spice them up a bit, but do leave them off if you prefer.

Serves 2

For the pitta crisps:

3 pitta breads

2 tbsp olive oil

1 tsp cumin seeds

1 tsp dried chilli flakes

Sea salt flakes & freshly ground black pepper

For the herb yogurt:

A generous handful of mixed fresh herbs, finely chopped (coriander, mint, parsley & chives are all good)

160g Greek yogurt

A little salt & freshly ground black pepper

For the Baghdad eggs:

2 tsp cumin seeds

50g unsalted butter

A splash of olive oil

2 cloves garlic, sliced

1 tsp paprika

4 eggs

Salt & freshly ground black pepper

Preheat the oven to 180°C/Gas 4.

Slice the pittas into 3cm-wide strips and peel apart the 2 layers of each strip. Place in a single layer on a baking tray, drizzle over the olive oil and scatter on the cumin seeds, chilli flakes and a generous seasoning of sea salt and black pepper. Bake in the oven for about 10 minutes until completely dry and crisp. Remove from the oven and allow to cool on a wire rack.

Make the yogurt sauce by stirring the herbs through the yogurt and seasoning to taste. Spoon on to two plates and set aside.

For the eggs, in a large frying pan dry-fry the cumin seeds for just a minute or so. As soon as you smell their aroma rising from the pan, tip them into a mortar and grind coarsely with the pestle. Add the butter to the pan, along with a drizzle of olive oil to help prevent it burning. When it has melted and starts foaming, stir through the garlic, paprika and ground cumin and fry for a couple of minutes. Then crack in the eggs and fry them, basting in the spiced butter until they are done to your liking.

When the eggs are cooked, use a fish slice to lift them out on to the serving plates, and drizzle over the butter. Serve immediately, with the pitta crisps to dunk in both the yolk and the yogurt.

29th January

Seville orange mousse with almond thins

Every year I welcome the arrival of the knobbly, thick-skinned Seville oranges into the greengrocer's. Some years I get around to making marmalade, and some years life feels too busy. But I still gain a small pleasure from just seeing them. For me they are a true

marker of the time of year, a clear signal that January will soon be February, as we inch slowly, slowly towards spring.

I have often thought it a shame that Sevilles were reserved almost exclusively for marmalade. Bitter and inedible raw, they do need to be cooked and sweetened considerably to make them palatable. This mousse was an experiment. I knew I wanted to harness their unique taste, as I felt it could offer something more complex than a standard orange. In the end I added the freshly grated zest of two clementines to the mousse; they added a floral citrus note that the Sevilles lacked. The result was a creamy, sharp and interestingly flavoured pudding that was a success even with the kids.

The almond thins are a doddle to make. You bake them flat in a large tray then cut them up after cooking. No messing around with rolling pins and cutters. What could be easier?

Serves 6–8

For the mousse:
2 Seville oranges, each cut into 6 wedges
500ml cold water
3 sheets of leaf gelatine
2 eggs
150g caster sugar
300ml double cream
Finely grated zest of 2 clementines

For the almond thins:
250g butter, softened
200g golden caster sugar
1 egg
250g plain flour
1 tsp vanilla extract
200g flaked almonds

Start the mousse by putting the orange wedges and water in a saucepan. Bring to the boil and cook, uncovered, for 20 minutes, prodding with a wooden spoon from time to time to release the juice from the flesh and the oils from the skin. Strain into a measuring jug. It should yield approximately 150ml orange juice – top up with a little cold water if it is slightly under. Set aside to cool for 5 minutes.

Soak the gelatine sheets in a shallow bowl of cold water for 5 minutes. Remove the sheets, squeeze out excess water and add to the orange juice, stirring until they dissolve.

Break the eggs into a large mixing bowl and stir the sugar into them. Set the bowl over a pan of barely simmering water, taking care there's no contact between bowl and water. Using an electric whisk, beat the egg and sugar until the mixture thickens and turns pale yellow. Turn off the whisk and lift it a little out of the bowl – if you trail it slightly above the mixture it should leave a thin ribbon in its wake. You can use a balloon whisk rather than an electric one but it will take a fair bit of work to get to this 'ribbon stage'. Pour in the double cream, orange juice and clementine zest and continue to whisk for a few moments until well combined. Transfer to a large serving bowl, or individual glasses if you fancy, and leave to set in the fridge. This will take 2–3 hours in a large bowl, or an hour or so in small glasses.

To make the biscuits, preheat the oven to 170°C/Gas 3. Beat the butter with the sugar in a food mixer until pale and fluffy. Add the egg, flour and vanilla extract, and beat again until a smooth paste is formed.

Line 2 baking trays with non-stick baking paper and scoop half the mixture on to the centre of each sheet. Use a spatula to spread the mix outwards in a thin layer until it covers the sheet. Sprinkle the almonds over evenly. Bake for about 15 minutes until a pale golden brown. Remove from the oven and, using a sharp knife, cut into squares. Leave to cool on the baking trays. Stored in an airtight tin, layered with baking paper, they will keep for several days.

1st February

Sublime onion tart

I often dream in ingredients, recipes and flavours, and this tart is just the kind of thing to feature in my nocturnal thoughts. It is one of those rare dishes that uses a mere handful of ingredients and yet tastes hugely complex. I would go as far as to say this is a frugal dish, albeit one of the best kinds. It takes a very cheap ingredient, onions, in bulk and adds a little luxury in the form of double cream. The resulting tart is deeply savoury, unctuous, and really rather wonderful on a cold winter's night.

We ate this tart lukewarm with a simple crisp green salad. It served two, with generous leftovers for lunch the next day. The onions seem to take on a more complex, sweet softness when served barely warm. But you can eat it hot if that's what you fancy. I wouldn't, however, eat it fridge-cold – the whole subtle, gentle, point of the dish would be lost.

Serves 4

For the pastry:
130g plain flour, plus extra for dusting

Fine sea salt

65g unsalted butter, cut into 1cm cubes

A few tablespoons ice-cold water

For the filling:
50g unsalted butter
900g white onions, sliced

2 sprigs fresh rosemary, needles picked & finely chopped

A splash of olive oil

200ml double cream

150ml milk

4 eggs

Salt & freshly ground black pepper

Begin by making the pastry. In a large bowl, season the flour with a little fine sea salt. Add the butter and rub into the flour, with cold fingers and a light touch, until it resembles breadcrumbs.

Alternatively, pulse in a food processor to achieve the same effect. Then add just enough water to bring the pastry together in a ball. This will be something like 3 tablespoons, maybe a little more, maybe a little less. If you overdo it and it ends up sticky, add a sprinkling of extra flour. Wrap tightly in clingfilm and chill in the fridge for 30 minutes.

For the filling, melt the butter very gently in a deep, wide frying pan, and add the onions, rosemary and a splash of oil. Cook as gently as possible for as long as possible – an hour would be good. The point of this tart is the melting, sublime onions, and this is a step that must not be rushed. A square of baking paper, scrunched up under a running tap then shaken, unfolded and tucked over the onions will provide a steamy lid that prevents the onions burning.

Preheat the oven to 180°C/Gas 4. While the onions are cooking, remove the pastry from the fridge. On a floured work surface, roll as thin as you dare, and use to line a loose-based 25cm flan tin. Prick the pastry bottom all over with a fork and line with baking paper and baking beans. Bake blind for 15–20 minutes, until the pastry is crisp and golden around the edges. Remove the paper and beans and return to the oven for 5 more minutes to dry out, then take out the pastry case and allow to cool. Turn the oven down to 160°C/Gas 3.

Lightly beat the cream and milk with the eggs and season with a little salt and plenty of black pepper. Spread the cooked onions over the pastry case and pour in the custard. Bake in the oven for around 35–40 minutes or until the filling is just set.

4th February

Lime meringue pie

I am so completely over winter now and have an almost painful longing to feel warm sun on bare skin. Enough of the thick scarves, itchy jumpers and permanently cold feet. I also want to begin to eat fresher, more sprightly things, yet I am not quite ready to give up the comfort food I've grown so used to over the past few months. Comfort eating to me is generally about celebrating fats in all their wonderful guises: rich creamy sauces wrapped around long ribbons of pasta, unctuous stews made with gelatinous cuts of meat, warming puddings generously dressed with sweet vanilla custard. So I dig deep into the freezer and look for the ever useful supplies of spring-green vegetables, the peas and the broad beans, that can usually be found there. I couple them with rich oozing cheeses, perhaps tossed into an omelette or stirred through a risotto, to produce a comforting winter meal that has a toe dipped into spring.

The transition from winter to spring is also reflected in the puddings I make. I feel the need to deliver something sweet and gentle, yet acid-sharp and lively. Lemon meringue pie, that childhood favourite, seems to fit the bill perfectly. But today I have no lemons, only limes, and it is to them I turn to create my winter-with-a-hint-of-spring Sunday pudding. I am proud to say I flicked through my copy of *Delia's Complete Cookery Course* for the basic recipe. Just as you can always rely on winter turning to spring, so you can rely on Delia. Her recipes work and that is the reason hers is one of the most well-thumbed books on my shelf. As well as substituting the limes for lemons, I tweaked the quantities to give an even thicker layer of citrus filling. The result was an overwhelming success. As my seven-year-old said: 'Mum, I just can't find the words to describe how amazing this is!' He went on to eat more than a quarter of the pie in a single sitting. Nothing makes this Mummy happier than seeing her children eating and enjoying their food as much as she does.

Serves 4–6, depending on greed

For the pastry:
110g plain flour
55g unsalted butter
2–3 tbsp cold water

For the filling:
400ml cold water
4 generous tbsp cornflour

75g caster sugar
Zest and juice of 5 ripe juicy limes
3 large egg yolks
70g unsalted butter

For the meringue:
3 large egg whites
165g caster sugar

To make the pastry, whiz the flour and butter in a food processor to form fine crumbs. Add just enough water to bring it together. Wrap in clingfilm and rest in the fridge for 20–30 minutes.

Preheat the oven to 190°C/Gas 5. Lightly grease a 23cm loose-based tart tin and roll the pastry into a circle big enough to line it. If it cracks a little, patch it up in the tin, using a little water if you need to stick it together. I find that the best, crumbliest pastry is often the least promising looking when you are working with it. Line with baking paper and baking beans and bake blind in the oven for 15–20 minutes until crisp and golden around the edges. Remove the paper and beans and return to the oven for 5 more minutes to dry out, then take out and allow to cool. Lower the heat to 150°C/Gas 2.

Next, prepare the filling. Measure the water into a jug. Put the cornflour and sugar into a bowl. Use enough of the water to make the cornflour into a paste, then pour the remainder into a pan with the lime zest. Bring up to the boil, then pour over the cornflour paste, stirring all the time until smooth. Pour the whole lot back into the saucepan and simmer for 1–2 minutes until thickened. Remove from the heat, add the egg yolks, lime juice and butter, and stir until combined. Pour the lime mixture into the pastry case and smooth with a knife. Set aside.

For the meringue, whisk the egg whites until they form stiff peaks. Add the sugar and carry on whisking until you have a thick glossy meringue. Using a wide knife, smooth the meringue over the lime filling, taking care to seal the edges. Add a few artistic swirls if you fancy. If you have a piping bag this could be the perfect opportunity to use it. Bake in the oven for around 35 minutes or until the meringue has turned a lovely golden beige. Remove from the oven and allow to go cold before eating.

9th February

Malaysian egg & aubergine curry with yellow spiced rice

Boiled eggs in a curry sauce are common across India and South-east Asia. I remember eating a delicious egg curry in Malaysia many years ago, and here is my interpretation of it. The curry paste is loosely based on a laksa and I make no claims to its authenticity but it did taste mighty good. Some of the ingredients – the galangal (an edible root similar to ginger), fresh turmeric, tamarind and lime leaves – can be tricky to find but an Asian grocery should stock them all. Once you have made the effort to seek them out, it's a good idea to buy plenty. Fresh root spices like ginger, galangal and turmeric freeze well – simply grate off what you need and return it to the freezer.

Serves 4

For the yellow spiced rice:

350g white long-grain rice – I used Thai jasmine rice

400ml coconut milk

300ml water

15g fresh turmeric, grated

Lemongrass trimmings from the spice paste

8 kaffir lime leaves (frozen are best)

For the spice paste:

1 tbsp coriander seeds

1 tsp black peppercorns

50g fresh ginger, chopped

35g fresh galangal, chopped

25g fresh turmeric, chopped

2 lemongrass stalks, outer leaves removed & finely chopped

1 tsp shrimp paste

1–3 tsp dried red chilli flakes, to taste

2 tbsp vegetable oil

For the curry:

2 tbsp vegetable oil

1 fat aubergine, chopped in 2cm pieces

300g shallots, sliced

5 cloves garlic, chopped

400ml coconut milk

500ml cold water

6 eggs

2 tbsp tamarind paste

Salt & freshly ground black pepper

A few fresh coriander leaves to garnish

For the rice, put all the ingredients in a heavy-based pan, stir well and leave to soak for 30 minutes. Then bring it up to the boil, stir once and add a tight-fitting lid. Set the timer and simmer for just 1 minute. Turn off the heat and set the timer for 12 minutes. Do not be tempted to remove the lid, simply leave it until the time is up, after which the rice should have absorbed all the coconut milk. Fluff up the rice with a fork, removing and discarding the spices.

For the spice paste, grind the coriander seeds and black pepper either in a spice mill or with a pestle and mortar, then tip into a food processor. Add the ginger, galangal, turmeric, lemongrass, shrimp paste, chilli flakes and oil. Process to a smooth paste, adding a tablespoon or so of water if it gets stuck in the bowl. Set aside.

Heat the oil for the curry in a deep frying pan and fry the aubergine over a high heat until a little golden and coloured at the edges. Resist the temptation to stir too often or you will lower the heat in the pan. Once the aubergine has coloured a little, add the shallots, garlic and the spice paste, and fry for a further 5 minutes. Pour in the coconut milk and water. Bring up to the boil, cover

with a lid and simmer for about 20–30 minutes until the aubergine is soft and tender.

While the curry is cooking, hard-boil the eggs. Put them into a pan and cover with cold water. Bring up to the boil, reduce the heat to a steady simmer and cook for 7 minutes. Drain. Run under cold water until cool enough to handle, then peel and slice in half.

Once the aubergine is cooked, stir through the tamarind paste and season to taste with salt and black pepper. Tuck the eggs into the curry, pushing them lightly under the surface, and simmer for a few more minutes until they are warmed.

Serve the curry spooned over the rice and scatter with a little coriander.

12th February
Rhubarb & almond streusel cake

I know I have said it before, but I love cake. Plain cake, fruity cake, fancy cake, kids' cake, grown-up cake. You name it. The only cakes I'm not too keen on are 'gloopy icing' cakes. You know the ones – where there is more icing than cake and it's all a bit sickly sweet, not to mention difficult to eat. So, here is the latest cake, slotting rather nicely into the grown-up category. This is a wonderful cake for dessert when you have friends to visit, and with a dollop of crème fraîche it is elevated swiftly into 'pudding' territory. But great too for afternoon tea, and also for my favourite time to eat cake – weekend breakfast with a mug of good coffee. There is really no need to feel we have to eat muesli on a Saturday morning. No need at all.

This is the second almond-based cake in the book and I make no apology for that. Almond-based cakes keep well for several days, and I love the dense, damp eggy-ness you get with almonds.

Serves about 6

400g rhubarb, cut into 3cm pieces

Zest and juice of 1 orange

30g granulated sugar

200g unsalted butter

200g caster sugar

4 eggs

200g ground almonds

50g plain flour

1 heaped tsp baking powder

For the streusel topping:

100g flaked almonds

40g dark brown sugar

1 tsp ground ginger

Preheat the oven to 180°C/Gas 4. Line the base of a 23cm springform tin with baking paper and brush a little melted butter around the sides.

Arrange the rhubarb in a single layer in a baking dish. Add the orange zest and juice and sprinkle the granulated sugar over the top. Bake for 15–20 minutes until soft. Remove from the oven and allow to cool a little.

Make the cake batter by creaming together the butter and caster sugar, either by hand with a wooden spoon and a lot of elbow grease or, as I did, in a food mixer. Add the eggs one at a time, beating well between each addition. Fold in the ground almonds, flour and baking powder. Pour into the prepared cake tin and level a little with a knife. Press the baked rhubarb pieces lightly into the surface, reserving the cooking juices. It will look like a lot of rhubarb but during cooking it will be enveloped beautifully within the cake. Bake in the oven for 30 minutes.

While the cake is baking, make the topping by mixing the reserved rhubarb juice with the flaked almonds, brown sugar and ground ginger. When the cake has had its initial baking, spread this mixture gently over the surface and return to the oven for about another 20 minutes. It is ready when a skewer inserted in the centre comes out cleanish.

Remove from the oven and allow to cool in the tin.

16th February

Pumpkin & pine nut sformato

A *sformato* is an Italian baked vegetable cake that could best be described as a cross between a firm soufflé and a pastry-less quiche. I first came across sformato recipes in the wonderful Italian cookery tome *The Silver Spoon*, which has many interesting versions. They can be made with all manner of vegetables, fennel, mushrooms and courgettes all being popular, but mine was designed specifically to use the very last wedge of pumpkin from last year's bumper crop. I am so thrilled with the variety I grew – Marina di Chioggia, each plant bearing several huge fruit with thick knobbly skin and almost luminous orange flesh – that I have saved a dozen seeds for planting again in a couple of weeks' time. That the cycle of storing, growing, harvesting and eating continues is immensely pleasing for this amateur gardener.

Quite rich and filling, this needed just a large bowl of lettuce as an accompaniment for supper. Although there were only two of us, it would easily serve four for supper. In our case the leftovers were earmarked for a lunch more interesting than a sandwich – it will keep quite happily in the fridge for a few days.

Serves 4

2 tbsp olive oil

1 onion, finely sliced

2–3 sprigs thyme, leaves picked

3 cloves garlic, crushed

1kg pumpkin, peeled & cut into 2–3cm cubes

150ml water

50g butter, plus extra for greasing

50g plain flour

500ml milk

A pinch of freshly grated nutmeg

Salt & freshly ground black pepper

60g Parmesan, finely grated

4 eggs, beaten

75g pine nuts

Heat the oil in a deep frying pan and sweat the onion with the thyme over a low heat until it begins to soften: about 10 minutes. Add the garlic and fry for a further minute before adding the pumpkin and water. Give everything a good stir then cover loosely with a layer of damp baking paper, creating a steamy tent under which the vegetables will cook. Fry gently for 20–30 minutes until soft, lifting off the baking paper every now and then and mashing up the pumpkin with the back of a wooden spoon. It may take a little more or less time depending on the size you cut the pumpkin – you want to end up with a slightly lumpy purée.

While the pumpkin is cooking, make a béchamel sauce by melting the butter in a heavy-based saucepan, then stirring the flour in to form a smooth roux. Allow it to cook for a minute or so before pouring in the milk in a steady stream, whisking constantly over a medium heat until the sauce is smooth and begins to thicken. Bring up to a steady simmer and cook for about 10 minutes, stirring from time to time, until the sauce is thick and glossy. Season generously with nutmeg, salt and black pepper. Stir through nearly all of the Parmesan, reserving a couple of tablespoons for sprinkling over the top.

Preheat the oven to 180°C/Gas 4 and prepare a 23cm springform tin by greasing the base and sides generously with butter, lining the base with baking paper if your tin has a tendency to stick.

Pour the béchamel sauce into the pumpkin purée and mix well. Allow it to cool for 2–3 minutes, then stir in the eggs and add about two-thirds of the pine nuts. Transfer to the tin and sprinkle the rest of the pine nuts and the reserved Parmesan over the top. Bake for about 50 minutes, until a skewer inserted into the centre comes out clean. Remove from the oven and allow to cool for a few minutes in the tin then slide a knife around the edge to release the sides and cut into wedges. It will cut and serve better if it is warm rather than oven-hot.

18th February

Marmalade Bakewells

The much-longed-for but short-lived Seville orange season is coming to a close and sadly I don't think I am going to find time to make any marmalade this year. Happily for me, my lovely 'cooking buddy' Jo made a batch and presented me with a jar yesterday. I adore marmalade and like it nice and sharp, the bits neither too big nor too slight. Marmalade is absolutely perfect for breakfast. You have to envy the clever devil who invented it! It is sweet enough to give the sugar kick so often needed first thing in the morning, but sharp and tart enough to wake up the taste buds and bring you alive. When teamed with a decent coffee it really is the perfect pick-me-up. But as much as I love it on toast, I am often thinking of other ways to showcase its charms, and these marmalade Bakewells turned out to be a very good use of my precious jar.

Makes 12 mini tarts

For the pastry:

160g plain flour, plus extra for dusting

80g butter, cut into cubes, plus extra for greasing

2 tbsp cold water

For the filling:

150g unsalted butter

150g ground almonds

150g caster sugar

2 eggs

12 scant tsp marmalade, either home-made or good quality bought

50g flaked almonds

To make the pastry, pulse together the flour and butter in a food processor until it resembles fine breadcrumbs. Add the cold water and pulse again until it just starts to come together. Tip on to a sheet of clingfilm and gently press into a rough ball. Wrap tightly and chill for 30 minutes in the fridge.

Preheat the oven to 180°C/Gas 4. Prepare a 12-hole jam-tart tin by greasing with a little butter.

Roll out the pastry on a floured work surface until it is approximately 3mm thick, then leave to rest for a few minutes while you prepare the filling. In a food processor, pulse together the butter, ground almonds and sugar until they resemble fine crumbs. Add the eggs and blend to a thick paste.

Cut out 12 circles from the pastry and gently line the tart tin. Place a scant teaspoon of marmalade in the base of each tart – don't be too generous as you need room for the filling. Add a dessertspoonful of filling to each, and level with the flat of a knife. Be generous with the almond paste and fill them right to the top. If you have any leftover filling, it freezes brilliantly, so save it for when you find you have a little spare pastry and you feel like making yourself a quick treat.

Sprinkle a few flaked almonds on top of each tart and bake in the oven for around 20 minutes until golden brown on top. Allow to cool a little in the tin before transferring to a cooling rack.

21st February

Pancake Day

This recipe was originally a third smaller in quantity but I could not believe how many pancakes my children ate in one sitting so I upped the size. Izaac ate six and Eve ate four, and so I was forced to make another half batch so the grown-ups could at least try some. And that was after they had told me they were full up after dinner, thus confirming my belief that children (and some adults) have an entirely separate 'pudding tummy', where there is generally room for a little pudding even when you are stuffed to the gunnels.

Before you begin, a quiet word about the first pancake. In my experience it almost always fails, so do not be disappointed if this happens to you. That seems to be the law of pancake-making, and I'm afraid I cannot offer you any solutions. Better just to accept it, safe in the knowledge that the second one will be better. I did make a concerted effort to flip my pancakes but admitted defeat after the first few near disasters, including a close shave involving the dog who was circling the kitchen like a hopeful black shark.

Makes about 16 pancakes

170g plain flour
A pinch of fine salt
3 eggs
400ml milk
40g butter, melted
A little unsalted butter or vegetable oil for cooking the pancakes

To serve:
Lemon wedges and caster sugar
Maple syrup
Jam or chocolate spread

Weigh the flour into a large mixing bowl and stir the salt into it. Make a well in the middle and crack in the eggs. Using a whisk, beat together to form a thick, and most likely lumpy, paste. Gradually pour in the milk, whisking vigorously until the lumps have gone and you are left with a smooth and fairly runny batter. Set aside to rest for 15 minutes or so. When you are ready to cook, whisk through the melted butter.

Heat a little butter or vegetable oil in a heavy frying pan until hot. Pour in a couple of tablespoons of batter, tipping the pan from side to side to spread the pancake out into a thin even layer. Cook for just a minute, then flip over and cook the other side for another 30 seconds or so. Slide on to a warm plate and repeat with the rest of the mixture. Serve the pancakes with the filling of your choice. For me it has to be lemon and sugar, but jam, chocolate spread and maple syrup are all popular in our house.

23rd February

Warm butterbean, beetroot & egg winter salad

This is just the sort of store-cupboard supper that saves my bacon on many an evening. After a long day at work, which in my case usually means lots of cooking for other people, the last thing I need is a trip to the shops to buy more food. I want something quick and effortless to fill me up and this certainly fitted the bill. I usually try to have a few things in the cupboard with which to knock up a warm salad. Today's version contained boiled eggs, a spicy chorizo sausage, a tin of beans and a vacuum pack of un-vinegary beetroot. All really useful things to have hanging around, for days when you cannot face shopping.

Serves 2

For the dressing:

3 tbsp extra virgin olive oil

1 tbsp sherry vinegar

1 tbsp Dijon mustard

1 tbsp clear honey

1 tbsp crème fraîche

2 shallots, very finely chopped

A handful of flat-leaf parsley, chopped

1 tbsp capers, roughly chopped

Salt & freshly ground black pepper

For the salad:

100g piece chorizo, cut into 5mm slices

1 leek, washed & sliced

1 x 400g tin butterbeans, drained & rinsed

1 pack ready-cooked beetroot (250g), drained and chopped

3 eggs

A couple of handfuls of salad leaves

Make the dressing by whisking all the ingredients together in a small bowl, seasoning to taste with salt and black pepper. Set aside.

Put the chorizo in a large frying pan and fry over a medium-high heat until golden and lightly crisp. Remove and set aside on a plate, covered loosely with foil to keep it warm.

Lower the heat and gently sweat the leek in the oil released by the chorizo, taking care not to burn it or it will take on a bitter taste. Cook until soft, about 10–15 minutes. Add the butterbeans and fry for a further minute or two to warm. Return the chorizo to the pan along with the beetroot and toss well to mix.

To cook the eggs, put them in a pan of cold water, covering them by about a centimetre. Bring to the boil, reduce the heat to a steady simmer and cook for 5 minutes. This will give you a boiled egg with a set white and nearly set yolk. If you prefer a runny yolk, cook for a minute less, or for hard-boiled cook for a minute more. Remove from the heat and run under cold water until cool enough to handle. Peel and cut in half.

Scatter the salad leaves over two plates, pile on the butterbean mixture and top with the halved eggs. Drizzle over the dressing and serve immediately.

26th February

Lemon curd

You won't believe how simple lemon curd is to make. Just fling it all in a pan and warm it gently over a low heat until it thickens, then pour into clean jars. Compared to the shop-bought stuff, the taste is phenomenal and, like me, you'll be cursing yourself you haven't done it before. Provided you store it in sterilized jars and in the fridge, it will last for several weeks. But I doubt it'll be there for that long.

Makes 3 jars

4 eggs

Juice & finely grated zest of 4
large lemons

370g caster sugar

250g unsalted butter, cut into
1cm cubes

1 tbsp cornflour

Begin by sterilizing 3 standard-sized jam jars. Preheat the oven
to 160°C/Gas 3. Wash both the jars and the lids in warm soapy
water and rinse well. Shake off the excess water and stand
in a baking tray. Slide into the oven and leave until they are
completely dry: about 20 minutes.

While the jars are sterilizing, put all the ingredients together in
a heavy-based saucepan. Set over a low heat and warm, whisking
gently but pretty much continuously until it thickens. This should
take around 15 minutes, give or take a minute here and there,
depending on the depth of your saucepan. You are looking for
a consistency like natural yogurt. The lemon curd will thicken a
little further on cooling.

Carefully pour the hot lemon curd into the clean hot jars and
screw the lid on tightly. Once cold, store in the fridge.

Index

Page numbers in **bold** denote an illustration

alioli, saffron 115–16
almond(s)
    almond, apricot & raspberry Danish 104–7, **105**
    chocolate-dipped nougat with candied orange, honey & 141–5, **142**
    citrus drizzle cake 238–9
    marmalade Bakewells 275–6
    peach & almond cake with lavender syrup 108–11, **109**
    plum, amaretto & almond crumble with vanilla custard 162–5, **163**
    rhubarb & almond streusel cake 269–71, **270**
    thins 259–60
amaretto
    plum, amaretto & almond crumble with vanilla custard 162–5, **163**
American breakfast pancakes 114–15
apples
    autumn apple & walnut cake 151–3
    blackberry & apple parfait with maple oat crumbs 136–9, **137**
    Eve's pudding 240–2, **241**
    toffee-apple doughnuts 193–6, **195**
apricot(s)
    almond, apricot & raspberry Danish 14–17, **105**
    and hazelnut roulade 47–50, **48**
April recipes 34–58
Armagnac
    far Breton with Armagnac prunes 207–9, **208**
Asian egg sarnie with carrot & cabbage 206–7
asparagus
    crispy bacon, asparagus & egg salad with creamy mustard dressing 53–6, **54**
    English 'Niçoise' of smoked trout, Jersey Royals and 88
    Greek lemon, egg & asparagus soup 72, **73**
    huevos revueltos with asparagus & prawns 64–6
aubergines
    beef & aubergine moussaka 202–4, **203**
    Malaysian egg & aubergine curry with yellow spiced rice 266–9, **268**
August recipes 123–45
autumn apple & walnut cake 151–3
avocado
    herby French toast with sun-blush tomatoes, avocado & crispy bacon 25–6

bacon
    bacon, parsnip & cheese brunch muffins 173–4
    crispy bacon, asparagus & egg salad with creamy mustard dressing 53–6, **54**
    & fried egg sarnie 77
    herby French toast with sun-blush tomatoes, avocado & crispy 25–6
    pasta 'carbonara' with cavolo nero 43–4, **44**
    smoked haddock chowder with poached eggs 210–11
Baghdad eggs with herb yogurt & pitta crisps 255–7, **256**
baked eggs with wild mushrooms and cream 190–2, **191**
baked rice pudding with greengages 132–3
Bakewells, marmalade 275–6
bananas
    coffee custard & 245–6
    spiced banana cake 107–8
beans
    broad bean, feta & mint omelette 121–3
    crisp cannellini bean & courgette fritters 111–14, **113**
    tonka bean ice cream **234**, 236–7
    warm butterbean, beetroot & egg winter salad 279–80
béarnaise sauce 45–7
beef
    & aubergine moussaka 202–4, **203**
    steak with béarnaise sauce 45–7
beetroot
    Russian salad 133–6, **134**
    warm butterbean, beetroot & egg winter salad 279–80
berries
    summer berries & cream shortcake 93–5, **94**
bhaji
    cauliflower bhaji with raita 175–7, **176**
birthday cakes 177–9
biscuits
    almond thins 259–60
bitter chocolate & cardamom ice cream **234**, 235–6
blackberry & apple parfait with maple oat crumbs 136–9, **137**
boiled eggs 196–7
bread
    brioche loaf 184–5

caramelized onion, Cheddar & rosemary scone 166–7
crispy bacon, asparagus & egg salad with creamy mustard dressing 53–5, **54**
herby French toast with sun-blush tomatoes, avocado & crispy bacon 25–6
watercress & brie flamiche 50–3, **52**
see also sandwiches
bread & butter pudding
    date, orange & pistachio 221–4, **222**
breadcrumbs
    Queen of puddings 101–2, **103**
brie
    watercress & brie flamiche 50–3, **52**
'brik', crab & egg 61–4, **62**
brioche loaf 184–5
broad bean, feta & mint omelette 121–3
broccoli
    purple sprouting broccoli with lemony hollandaise 31–2
butterbeans
    warm butterbean, beetroot & egg winter salad 279–80
buttercream, lemon 178–9

cabbage
    Asian egg sarnie with carrot & 206–7
Caerphilly
    omelette with Caerphilly & wild garlic 20–2, **21**
cakes
    autumn apple & walnut 151–3
    birthday 177–9
    chocolate & walnut torte 250–2, **251**
    citrus drizzle 238–9
    coffee & walnut 58–61, **59**
    far Breton with Armagnac prunes 207–9, **208**
    fig & oloroso upside-down 67–9, **68**
    peach & almond cake with lavender syrup 108–11, **109**
    rhubarb & almond streusel 269–71, **270**
    spiced banana 107–8
    summer berries & cream shortcake 93–5, **94**
candied orange 143
cannellini beans
    crisp cannellini bean & courgette fritters 111–14, **113**
capers
    red pepper & goat's cheese tart 123–6, **125**

Russian salad 133–6, **134**
salsa verde 232–3
caramelized onion, Cheddar &
rosemary scone bread 166–7
cardamom
bitter chocolate & cardamom ice
cream **234**, 235–6
carrot(s)
Asian egg sarnie with carrot &
cabbage 206–7
& cumin tart 185–7
cauliflower bhaji with raita 175–7, **176**
cavolo nero
nasi goreng with nam prik sauce
252–4
pasta 'carbonara' with 43–5, **44**
chakchouka with merguez sausages &
baked eggs 181–3, **182**
Cheddar
caramelized onion, Cheddar &
rosemary scone bread 166–7
& wholegrain mustard croquetas
157–9, **158**
cheese
bacon, parsnip & cheese brunch
muffins 173–4
beef & aubergine moussaka 202–4,
203
broad bean, feta & mint omelette
121–3
caramelized onion, Cheddar &
rosemary scone bread 166–7
carrot & cumin tart 185–7
Cheddar & wholegrain mustard
croquetas 157–9, **158**
crisp cannellini bean & courgette
fritters 111–14, **113**
Florentine-style spinach and egg
tarts 85–7, **86**
gougères with creamed leeks &
cider-braised gammon 246–9, **247**
omelette with Caerphilly & wild
garlic 20–2, **21**
pasta 'carbonara' with cavolo nero
43–5, **44**
red pepper & goat's cheese tart
123–6, **125**
sage tagliatelle with roast pumpkin
& Stilton 170–3, **171**
salami, pesto & ricotta frittata
149–50
smoked salmon & chive soufflé 16–17
& tomato scrambled egg 153–4, **155**
watercress & brie flamiche 50–3, **52**
wild garlic, spinach & pecorino
gnocchi with tomato sauce 34–6
cheesecake
Italian pear & ginger baked 167–9,
168
lemon cheesecake with raspberries
126–8
chickpeas
falafel eggs **129**, 131–2

chillies
cauliflower bhaji with raita 175–7,
176
crab & egg 'brik' 61–4, **62**
Indian spiced potato pancakes with
coriander & tomato chutney
74–6, **75**
nasi goreng with nam prik sauce
252–4
stir-fried vegetable noodles with
chilli egg & soy salmon 70–1
Chinese egg & prawn custard, with
stir-fried greens and rice 26–9, **27**
chives
salsa verde 232–3
smoked salmon & chive soufflé
16–17
chocolate
-dipped nougat with candied orange,
honey & almonds 141–5, **142**
bitter chocolate & cardamom ice
cream **234**, 235–6
mocha éclairs 23–4
& walnut torte 250–2, **251**
chorizo
gala pie with 89–92, **90**
warm butterbean, beetroot & egg
winter salad 279–80
chowder
smoked haddock chowder with
poached eggs 210–11
Christmas ham, egg & salsa verde
sandwich 230–3, **231**
Christmas pudding 214–17, **215**
chutney
Indian spiced potato pancakes with
coriander & tomato 74–6, **75**
cider
gougères with creamed leeks &
cider-braised gammon 246–9, **247**
cinnamon
Spanish flan 179–81
citrus drizzle cake 238–9
clafoutis, gooseberry & elderflower
120–1
coconut marshmallows 187–90, **188**
coffee
custard & bananas 245–6
mocha éclairs 23–4
& walnut cake 58–61, **59**
coriander
Indian spiced potato pancakes with
coriander & tomato chutney 74–6,
75
courgette(s)
crisp cannellini bean & courgette
fritters 111–14, **113**
& lime muffins 156–7
pea, yellow courgette & mint quiche
117–19, **118**
crab
& egg 'brik' 61–4, **62**
with mayonnaise 81–3

cream
apricot and hazelnut roulade 47–50,
48
baked eggs with wild mushrooms
and 190–2, **191**
crème brûlée 217–19
gougères with creamed leeks &
cider-braised gammon 246–9, **247**
mocha éclairs 23–4
quince, Marsala and lemon trifle
197–200
rhubarb & rosewater pavlova 17–20,
18
Spanish flan 179–81
spiced nut meringues with Marsala
224–6
summer berries & cream shortcake
93–5, **94**
cream cheese
lemon cheesecake with raspberries
126–8
smoked salmon & chive soufflé
16–17
crème brûlée 217–19
crème caramel with a hint of orange &
cinnamon 179–81
crème fraîche
lemon cheesecake with raspberries
126–8
pasta 'carbonara' with cavolo nero
43–5, **44**
Russian salad 133–6, **134**
watercress & brie flamiche 50–3, **52**
crevettes, saffron alioli with 115–16
crisp cannellini bean & courgette
fritters 111–14, **113**
crisps, pitta 255–7, **256**
crispy bacon, asparagus & egg salad
with creamy mustard dressing 53–6, **54**
croquetas, Cheddar & wholegrain
mustard 157–9, **158**
crumble
plum, amaretto & almond crumble
with vanilla custard 162–5, **163**
cucumber
raita 175–7
cumin seeds
Baghdad eggs with herb yogurt &
pitta crisps 255–7, **256**
carrot & cumin tart 185–7
cauliflower bhaji with raita 175–7,
176
falafel eggs **129**, 131–2
currants
vanilla ice cream with warm currant
sauce 83–5
curried egg mayonnaise 139–41
curry
Malaysian egg & aubergine curry
with yellow spiced rice 266–9, **268**
custard
Chinese egg & prawn custard, with
stir-fried greens and rice 26–9, **27**

coffee custard & bananas 245–6
plum, amaretto & almond crumble
with vanilla 162–5, **163**
Portuguese custard tarts 13–15, **14**
quince, Marsala and lemon trifle
197–200
rhubarb & custard tart 40–2

Danish
almond, apricot & raspberry 104–7,
105
dates
date, orange & pistachio bread &
butter pudding 221–4, **222**
sticky toffee pudding 29–31
December recipes 214–37
desserts
apricot and hazelnut roulade 47–50,
48
baked rice pudding with greengages
132–3
bitter chocolate & cardamom ice
cream **234**, 235–6
blackberry & apple parfait with
maple oat crumbs 136–9, **137**
coffee custard & bananas 245–6
crème brûlée 217–19
date, orange & pistachio bread &
butter pudding 221–4, **222**
Eve's pudding 240–2, **241**
gooseberry & elderflower clafoutis
120–1
Italian pear & ginger baked
cheesecake 167–9, **168**
lemon cheesecake with raspberries
126–8
lime meringue pie 264–6
orange flower water sorbet **234**, 237
pancakes 276–8
plum, amaretto & almond crumble
with vanilla custard 162–5, **163**
Queen of puddings 101–2, **103**
quince, Marsala and lemon trifle
197–200
rhubarb & custard tart 40–2
rhubarb & rosewater pavlova 17–20,
18
Seville orange mousse with almond
thins 257–60, **258**
Spanish flan 179–81
spiced nut meringues with Marsala
cream 224–6
stem ginger, raisin & whisky
steamed pudding 56–8
sticky toffee pudding 29–31
tonka bean ice cream **234**, 236–7
vanilla ice cream with warm currant
sauce 83–5
doughnuts, toffee-apple 193–6, **195**
dressing, creamy mustard 53–5, **54**

éclairs, mocha 23–4
egg mayonnaise 139–41

egg toast, Korean 206–7
elderflower
gooseberry & elderflower clafoutis
120–1
empanada gallega 98–101, **99**
English 'Niçoise' of smoked trout,
Jersey Royals and asparagus 88
Eve's pudding 240–2, **241**

falafel eggs **129**, 131–2
far Breton with Armagnac prunes
207–9, **208**
February recipes 261–82
festive rabbit & prune pâté 226–9, **227**
feta cheese
broad bean, feta & mint omelette
121–3
fig(s)
Christmas pudding 214–17
& oloroso upside-down cake 67–9, **68**
filo pastry
crab & egg 'brik' 61–4, **62**
flamiche, watercress & brie 50–3, **52**
flan, Spanish 179–81
Florentine-style spinach and egg tarts
85–7, **86**
fondant icing 178–9
French toast
herby French toast with sun-blush
tomatoes, avocado & crispy bacon
25–6
fried eggs
bacon & fried egg sarnie 77
Baghdad eggs with herb yogurt &
pitta crisps 255–7, **256**
nasi goreng with nam prik sauce
252–4
frittata
salami, pesto & ricotta 149–50
fritters, crisp cannellini bean &
courgette 111–14, **113**

gala pie with chorizo 89–92, **90**
gammon
gala pie with chorizo 89–92, **90**
gougères with creamed leeks &
cider-braised 246–9, **247**
garlic
omelette with Caerphilly & wild
20–2, **21**
saffron aïoli 115–16
wild garlic, spinach & pecorino
gnocchi with tomato sauce 34–6
ginger
Italian pear & ginger baked
cheesecake 167–9, **168**
stem ginger, raisin & whisky
steamed pudding 56–8
gnocchi
wild garlic, spinach & pecorino
gnocchi with tomato sauce 34–6

goat's cheese
red pepper & goat's cheese tart
123–6, **125**
gooseberry & elderflower clafoutis
120–1
gougère
cheese gougères with creamed leeks
& cider-braised gammon 246–9,
247
Greek lemon, egg & asparagus soup
72, **73**
green beans
Russian salad 133–6, **134**
green lentils
pumpkin & green lentil moussaka
204–5
greengages, baked rice pudding with
132–3
greens *see* spring greens

haddock *see* smoked haddock
ham
Christmas ham, egg & salsa verde
sandwich 230–3, **231**
hard-boiled eggs 196–7
hazelnuts
apricot and hazelnut roulade 47–50,
48
herby French toast with sun-blush
tomatoes, avocado & crispy bacon
25–6
hollandaise sauce, purple sprouting
broccoli with lemony 31–2
honey
chocolate-dipped nougat with
candied orange, honey & almonds
141–5, **142**
hot cross buns 37–9, **38**
huevos revueltos with asparagus &
prawns 64–6

ice cream 233, 235
bitter chocolate & cardamom **234**,
235–6
tonka bean **234**, 236–7
vanilla ice cream with warm currant
sauce 83–5
icing, pink fondant 178–9
Indian spiced potato pancakes with
coriander & tomato chutney 74–6, **75**
Italian pear & ginger baked cheesecake
167–9, **168**

January recipes 238–60
July recipes 104–23
June recipes 81–102

kedgeree with poached eggs 242–4
Korean egg toast 206–7

lavender flowers
peach & almond cake with lavender
syrup 108–11, **109**

leeks
  gougères with creamed leeks &
    cider-braised gammon 246–9, **247**
  kedgeree with poached eggs 242–4
  smoked haddock chowder with
    poached eggs 210–11
  watercress & brie flamiche 50–3, **52**
lemon(s)
  buttercream 178–9
  cheesecake with raspberries 126–8
  citrus drizzle cake 238–9
  curd 280–2, **281**
  Greek lemon, egg & asparagus soup
    72, **73**
  purple sprouting broccoli with
    lemony hollandaise 31–2
  quince, Marsala and lemon trifle
    197–200
lentils
  pumpkin & green lentil moussaka
    204–5
lime(s)
  citrus drizzle cake 238–9
  courgette & lime muffins 156–7
  meringue pie 264–6
  mojito sorbet 160–2, **161**

Malaysian egg & aubergine curry with
  yellow spiced rice 266–9, **268**
maple syrup
  blackberry & apple parfait with
    maple oat crumbs 136–9, **137**
March recipes 13–32
marmalade Bakewells 275–6
Marsala
  pasta 'carbonara' with cavolo nero
    43–5, **44**
  quince, Marsala and lemon trifle
    197–200
  spiced nut meringues with Marsala
    cream 224–6
marshmallows
  coconut marshmallows 187–90, **188**
mascarpone
  Italian pear & ginger baked
    cheesecake 167–9, **168**
  smoked salmon & chive soufflé 16–17
May recipes 58–77
mayonnaise
  basic recipe 81–3, **82**
  curried egg 139–41
  Russian salad 133–6, **134**
  saffron alioli 115–16
merguez sausages
  chakchouka with merguez sausages
    & baked eggs 181–3, **182**
meringue(s)
  lime meringue pie 264–6
  Queen of puddings 101–2, **103**
  rhubarb & rosewater pavlova 17–20,
    18
  spiced nut meringues with Marsala
    cream 224–6

milk
  baked rice pudding with greengages
    132–3
  Cheddar & wholegrain mustard
    croquetas 157–9, **158**
  date, orange & pistachio bread &
    butter pudding 221–4, **222**
  Queen of puddings 101–2, **103**
  smoked haddock chowder with
    poached eggs 210–11
mint
  broad bean, feta & mint omelette
    121–3
  mojito sorbet 160–2, **161**
  pea, yellow courgette & mint quiche
    117–19, **118**
  raita 175–7
  salsa verde 232–3
  mocha éclairs 23–4
  mojito sorbet 160–2, **161**
moussaka 200
  beef & aubergine 202–4, **203**
  pumpkin & green lentil 204–5
mousse
  Seville orange mousse with almond
    thins 257–60, **258**
muffins
  bacon, parsnip & cheese brunch 173–4
  courgette & lime 156–7
mushrooms
  baked eggs with wild mushrooms
    and cream 190–2, **191**
  Chinese egg & prawn custard, with
    stir-fried greens and rice 26–9, **27**
  nasi goreng with nam prik sauce
    252–4
  stir-fried vegetable noodles with
    chilli egg & soy salmon 70–1
mustard
  Cheddar & wholegrain mustard
    croquetas 157–9, **158**
  crispy bacon, asparagus & egg salad
    with creamy mustard dressing
    53–6, **54**

nam prik sauce 252–4
nasi goreng with nam prik sauce 252–4
noodles
  stir-fried vegetable noodles with
    chilli egg & soy salmon 70–1
nougat
  chocolate-dipped nougat with
    candied orange, honey & almonds
    141–5, **142**
November recipes 190–211
nuts
  apricot and hazelnut roulade 47–50,
    48
  autumn apple & walnut cake 151–3
  chocolate & walnut torte 250–2, **251**
  coffee & walnut cake 58–61, **59**
  date, orange & pistachio bread &
    butter pudding 221–4, **222**

pumpkin & pine nut sformato 272–4
spiced nut meringues with Marsala
  cream 224–65

oats
  blackberry & apple parfait with
    maple oat crumbs 136–9, **137**
October recipes 170–90
oloroso sherry
  fig & oloroso upside-down cake
    67–9, **68**
omelette(s)
  broad bean, feta & mint 121–3
  with Caerphilly & wild garlic 20–2,
    21
  salami, pesto & ricotta frittata 149–50
  tortilla española with smoky tomato
    sauce 96–8
onion(s)
  caramelized onion, Cheddar &
    rosemary scone bread 166–7
  tart 261–3
  tuna, egg & sweet pepper pie
    98–101, **99**
  Yorkshire pudding with spring
    greens, sausages & caramelized
    shallot gravy 219–21
orange flower water sorbet **234**, 237
oranges
  chocolate-dipped nougat with
    candied orange, honey & almonds
    141–5, **142**
  citrus drizzle cake 238–9
  date, orange & pistachio bread &
    butter pudding 221–4, **222**
  orange flower water sorbet **234**, 237
  Seville orange mousse with almond
    thins 257–60, **258**
  Spanish flan 179–81

pak choi
  stir-fried vegetable noodles with
    chilli egg & soy salmon 70–1
pancakes
  American breakfast 114–15
  basic recipe 276–8
  Indian spiced potato pancakes with
    coriander & tomato chutney
    74–6, **75**
parfait
  blackberry & apple parfait with
    maple oat crumbs 136–9, **137**
Parmesan
  crisp cannellini bean & courgette
    fritters 111–14, **113**
  pasta 'carbonara' with cavolo nero
    43–5, **44**
parsley
  crab & egg 'brik' 61–4, **62**
  salsa verde 232–3
parsnips
  bacon, parsnip & cheese brunch
    muffins 173–4

pasta
'carbonara' with cavolo nero 43–5, 44
sage tagliatelle with roast pumpkin
& Stilton 170–3, **171**
pastéis de Belém 13–15, **14**
pastry
almond, apricot & raspberry Danish
104–7, **105**
carrot & cumin tart 185–7
crab & egg 'brik' 61–4, **62**
Florentine-style spinach and egg
tarts 85–7, **86**
Gala pie with chorizo 89–92, **90**
gougères with creamed leeks &
cider-braised gammon 246–9, **247**
lime meringue pie 264–6
marmalade Bakewells 275–6
onion tart 261–3
Portuguese custard tarts 13–15, **14**
red pepper & goat's cheese tart
123–6, **125**
rhubarb & custard tart 40–2
tuna, egg & sweet pepper pie
98–101, **99**
pâté, festive rabbit & prune 226–9, **227**
pavlova, rhubarb & rosewater 17–20,
18
peach & almond cake with lavender
syrup 108–11, **109**
pears
Italian pear & ginger baked
cheesecake 167–9, **168**
pea, yellow courgette & mint quiche
117–19, **118**
pecorino cheese
wild garlic, spinach & pecorino
gnocchi with tomato sauce 34–6
peppers
chakchouka with merguez sausages
& baked eggs 181–3, **182**
red pepper & goat's cheese tart
123–6, **125**
tuna, egg & sweet pepper pie
98–101, **99**
pesto
salami, pesto & ricotta frittata
149–50
pie
gala pie with chorizo 89–92, **90**
lime meringue 264–6
tuna, egg & sweet pepper 98–101,
99
pine nuts
pumpkin & pine nut sformato 272–4
salami, pesto & ricotta frittata
149–50
pink fondant icing 178–9
pistachios
date, orange & pistachio bread &
butter pudding 221–4, **222**
pitta crisps 255–7, **256**
plum, amaretto & almond crumble with
vanilla custard 162–5, **163**

poached eggs
kedgeree with 242–4
smoked haddock chowder with
210–11
pork
gala pie with chorizo 89–92, **90**
Portuguese custard tarts 13–15, **14**
potatoes
English 'Niçoise' of smoked trout,
Jersey Royals and asparagus 88
Indian spiced potato pancakes with
coriander & tomato chutney
74–6, **75**
Russian salad 133–6, **134**
smoked haddock chowder with
poached eggs 210–11
tortilla española with smoky tomato
sauce 96–8
prawns
Chinese egg & prawn custard, with
stir-fried greens and rice 26–9, **27**
huevos revueltos with asparagus &
64–6
nasi goreng with nam prik sauce
252–4
saffron alioli with crevettes 115–16
prunes
far Breton with Armagnac 207–9,
208
festive rabbit & prune pâté 226–9,
227
pumpkin
& green lentil moussaka 204–5
& pine nut sformato 272–4
sage tagliatelle with roast pumpkin
& Stilton 170–3, **171**
purple sprouting broccoli with lemony
hollandaise 31–2

Queen of puddings 101–2, **103**
quiche
carrot & cumin tart 185–7
pea, yellow courgette & mint
117–19, **118**
red pepper & goat's cheese tart
123–6, **125**
quince, Marsala and lemon trifle
197–200

rabbit
festive rabbit & prune pâté 226–9, **227**
raisins
Christmas pudding 214–17, **215**
spiced banana cake 107–8
stem ginger, raisin & whisky
steamed pudding 56–8
raita, cauliflower bhaji with 175–7, **176**
raspberries
almond, apricot & raspberry Danish
104–7, **105**
lemon cheesecake with 126–8
summer berries & cream shortcake
93–5, **94**

red pepper & goat's cheese tart 123–6,
125
rhubarb
& almond streusel cake 269–71, **270**
& custard tart 40–2
& rosewater pavlova 17–20, **18**
rice
Chinese egg & prawn custard, with
stir-fried greens and rice 26–9, **27**
kedgeree with poached eggs 242–4
Malaysian egg & aubergine curry
with yellow spiced 266–9, **268**
nasi goreng with nam prik sauce
252–4
rice pudding
baked rice pudding with greengages
132–3
ricotta cheese
Italian pear & ginger baked
cheesecake 167–9, **168**
salami, pesto & ricotta frittata
149–50
wild garlic, spinach & pecorino
gnocchi with tomato sauce 34–6
rosemary
caramelized onion, Cheddar &
rosemary scone bread 166–7
rosewater
rhubarb & rosewater pavlova 17–20,
18
roulade, apricot and hazelnut 47–50, **48**
rum
mojito sorbet 160–2, **161**
Russian salad 133–6, **134**

saffron alioli 115–16
sage tagliatelle with roast pumpkin &
Stilton 170–3, **171**
salads
crispy bacon, asparagus & egg salad
with creamy mustard dressing
53–6, **54**
English 'Niçoise' of smoked trout,
Jersey Royals and asparagus 88
Russian 133–6, **134**
warm butterbean, beetroot & egg
winter 279–80
salami, pesto & ricotta frittata 149–50
salmon
stir-fried vegetable noodles with chilli
egg & soy 70–1
see also smoked salmon
salsa verde
Christmas ham, egg & salsa verde
sandwich 230–3, **231**
salt & pepper scotch eggs 130–1
sandwiches
Asian egg sarnie with carrot &
cabbage 206–7
bacon & fried egg 77
Christmas ham, egg & salsa verde
230–3, **231**
curried egg mayonnaise 139–41

sauces
béarnaise 45–7
currant 83–5
lemony hollandaise 31–2
mayonnaise 81–3, **82**
nam prik 252–4
saffron alioli 115–16
salsa verde 230–3
smoky tomato 96–8
tomato 34–6
sausages
chakchouka with merguez sausages
& baked eggs 181–3, **182**
Yorkshire pudding with spring
greens, sausages & caramelized
shallot gravy 219–21
sausagemeat
salt & pepper scotch eggs 130–1
scone bread, caramelized onion,
Cheddar & rosemary 166–7
scotch eggs
falafel eggs **129**, 131–2
salt & pepper 130–1
scrambled eggs
cheese & tomato 153–4, **155**
huevos revueltos with asparagus &
prawns 64–6
with smoked salmon 229–30
September recipes 149–69
Seville orange mousse with almond
thins 257–60, **258**
sformato, pumpkin & pine nut 272–4
shallots
Yorkshire pudding with spring
greens, sausages & caramelized
shallot gravy 219–21
sherry
baked eggs with wild mushrooms
and 190–2, **191**
fig & oloroso upside-down cake
67–9, **68**
shortcake, summer berries & cream
93–5, **94**
smoked haddock
chowder with poached eggs 210–11
kedgeree with poached eggs 242–4
smoked salmon
& chive soufflé 16–17
scrambled egg with 229–30
smoked trout
English 'Niçoise' of smoked trout,
Jersey Royals and asparagus 88
sorbet 235
mojito 160–2, **161**
orange flower water **234**, 237
soufflé, smoked salmon & chive 16–17
soups
Greek lemon, egg & asparagus 72,
73
see also chowder
soy sauce
stir-fried vegetable noodles with
chilli egg & soy salmon 70–1

Spanish flan 179–81
spiced banana cake 107–8
spiced nut meringues with Marsala
cream 224–6
spinach
Florentine-style spinach and egg
tarts 85–7, **86**
kedgeree with poached eggs 242–4
wild garlic, spinach & pecorino
gnocchi with tomato sauce 34–6
spring greens
Chinese egg & prawn custard, with
stir-fried greens and rice 26–9, **27**
nasi goreng with nam prik sauce
252–4
Yorkshire pudding with spring
greens, sausages & caramelized
shallot gravy 219–21
steamed pudding, stem ginger, raisin &
whisky 56–8
stem ginger, raisin & whisky steamed
pudding 56–8
stews
chakchouka with merguez sausages
& baked eggs 181–3, **182**
sticky toffee pudding 29–31
Stilton
sage tagliatelle with roast pumpkin
& 170–3, **171**
stir-fried vegetable noodles with chilli
egg & soy salmon 70–1
strawberries
summer berries & cream shortcake
93–5, **94**
summer berries & cream shortcake
93–5, **94**

tagliatelle
sage tagliatelle with roast pumpkin
& Stilton 170–3, **171**
tart(s)
carrot & cumin 185–7
Florentine-style spinach and egg
85–7, **86**
marmalade Bakewells 275–6
onion 261–3
Portuguese custard 13–15, **14**
red pepper & goat's cheese 123–6,
125
rhubarb & custard 40–2
toffee
-apple doughnuts 193–6, **195**
sticky toffee pudding 29–31
tomatoes
beef & aubergine moussaka 202–4,
203
chakchouka with merguez sausages
& baked eggs 181–3, **182**
cheese & tomato scrambled egg
153–4, **155**
herby French toast with sun-blush
tomatoes, avocado & crispy bacon
25–6

Indian spiced potato pancakes with
coriander & tomato chutney
74–6, **75**
red pepper & goat's cheese tart
123–6, **125**
tortilla española with smoky tomato
sauce 96–8
wild garlic, spinach & pecorino
gnocchi with tomato sauce 34–6
tonka bean ice cream **234**, 236–7
torte, chocolate & walnut 250–2, **251**
tortilla española with smoky tomato
sauce 96–8
trifle
quince, Marsala and lemon 197–200
trout *see* smoked trout
tuna, egg & sweet pepper pie 98–101,
99

vanilla
crème brûlée 217–19
ice cream with warm currant sauce
83–5
plum, amaretto & almond crumble
with vanilla custard 162–5, **163**

walnuts
autumn apple & walnut cake 151–3
chocolate & walnut torte 250–2, **251**
coffee & walnut cake 58–61, **59**
spiced banana cake 107–8
warm brioche 184–5
warm butterbean, beetroot & egg
winter salad 279–80
watercress & brie flamiche 50–3, **52**
whisky
stem ginger, raisin & whisky
steamed pudding 56–8
wild garlic
omelette with Caerphilly & wild
garlic 20–2, **21**
spinach & pecorino gnocchi with
tomato sauce 34–6

yogurt
bacon, parsnip & cheese brunch
muffins 173–4
Baghdad eggs with herb yogurt &
pitta crisps 255–7, **256**
raita 175–7
rhubarb & rosewater pavlova 17–20,
18
Yorkshire pudding with spring greens,
sausages & caramelized shallot gravy
219–21